Megaphones
Be With You

How Your Organization Can Play the Media Relations Game—and Win

Debbie Graham Fitzgerald and Ed Van Herik

Dedication

We dedicate this book to:

All of the colleagues we've had the privilege of working with and learning from—we enjoy the collaboration and laughter;

All of the clients we have worked with—we are grateful for your business, professionalism and friendship;

All of the media professionals we have worked with throughout the years—we are always amazed by your talent;

Our spouses who were with us when we created the title of the book (Can you say the title using a Darth Vadar accent?) and supported us through the lengthy process of writing;

Our families for their continued love.

About the Authors

Debbie Graham Fitzgerald

Debbie Graham Fitzgerald, a childhood soccer player who still keeps her cleats primed for a friendly scrimmage, has ignited fans with a megaphone in hand since her days as a college cheerleader captain at California Polytechnic State University, San Luis Obispo, California. She majored in business with a concentration in marketing, and, with her love of storytelling, minored in theatre. While she enjoyed her time in the spotlight, Debbie has since found a greater sense of purpose in championing others so they would shine.

She first put her fan-building skills to work at the William Morris Agency in Beverly Hills, California, where Debbie helped actors, including some celebrities, land gigs. Moving up the ranks in different firms over the years—from Marketing Assistant to Director of Marketing to Senior VP—she is now President of Fitzgerald PR Inc., a full-service, Atlanta-based PR agency Debbie launched with her husband, Tim, in 2003.

Devoted to her profession, Debbie serves on the board of the Georgia Chapter of the national Public Relations Society of America (PRSA), which is PRSA's second largest chapter with more than 800 members. She is also highly involved in PRSA through the organization's Georgia Independent Counselors special interest group, a small segment of PR practitioners and boutique PR firms that are dedicated to facilitating meaningful relationships among professional peers and promoting best practices. She has, in turn, been honored by PRSA Georgia for her contributions to the Chapter and awarded over the years for her outstanding work on behalf of clients.

In addition to generating publicity and developing a fan base for her clients, Debbie further raises awareness for important causes. She and Tim are also the No. 1 fans of their children, Megan and Charlie, budding athletes who know they can count on their mom's enthusiasm, whether as cheerleader or coach.

Ed Van Herik

After graduating from DePaul University, Ed Van Herik began a long career as a newspaper reporter and editor, working at papers including the *Dixon (Ill.) Evening Telegraph,* the *Roanoke Times,* the *Cleveland Plain Dealer,* the *Chicago Daily News* and the *Los Angeles Daily News.*

He also worked for two years as managing editor of *Crain's Cleveland Business,* later transitioning into public relations in Southern California.

Ed worked extensively promoting solar power and electric transportation for Southern California Edison before going to San Diego Gas & Electric, where he was the company's principal TV spokesperson during the California Energy Crisis of 2000-2001.

He relocated to Atlanta to be closer to his son and his family, starting his own full-service boutique agency, Van Herik Communications, in 2007.

Ed has received a number of public relations awards for service to clients, including one for keeping a controversial project in perspective within the community. He is active in the Georgia chapter of the Public Relations Society of America and talks frequently with other professionals to take advantage of emerging techniques.

Ed has been a jock since his college days, concentrating on sports like weightlifting, scuba diving, and whitewater rafting. From personal experience, he can highly recommend tai chi as a stress-reliever during a crisis.

Table of Contents

Introduction

A good media relations person is like a gifted cheerleading captain. By keeping an eye on the game and taking the pulse of the crowd, that person knows just how to work the megaphone. Choosing exactly the right cheer, a savvy captain engages the fans and energizes the team at the perfect time. Beyond creating a memorable, magical moment—everyone in the stands chanting as the star player (or the unexpected kid who typically warms the bench) charges towards the goal to score—the orchestrated event produces team pride and loyalty.

Did you ever wish you could work some media magic with a megaphone? Or do you feel like you're shouting into an empty stadium?

- Perhaps your competitor is the one consistently cited as the expert in prominent publications.

- Maybe you watch in awe as the media arrives in droves when the other organization hosts events.

- Or do their executives sound like heroes in the news, while your innovations go unnoticed?

If you haven't figured out how to reach your fans, much less gain any control over the message, you are like most businesses and nonprofits that are new to public relations. To be truthful, seasoned pros agree that the rules are confusing and scoring is tough. Even those of us who write books on the topic find the realm of media relations—orchestrating a cooperative effort with various media sources—challenging. No wonder PR novices, who are savvy about many other aspects of business, commonly have the same general yet important questions:

- Where do I start?
- Do I need to follow certain rules?
- What strategy will work for me?
- What can I do that I haven't been doing?
- Can I accomplish the job internally?
- Should I hire a professional?
- What is the investment and what's the return?

This book is meant to answer those questions for those in charge of any organization. You'll also gain a solid understanding of whether or not pursuing a media relations campaign is worth your effort at all.

Without a doubt, the megaphone can be a powerful communications tool in the right hands; therefore, to highlight particular topics, we present a megaphone icon each time we offer an example of media relations at work or an additional personal thought on the topic. (Note: We protect our current and former clients with confidentiality agreements and therefore do not divulge their names within our megaphone examples.)

In the end, you'll have a better understanding of the media relations game and how well this particular approach to garnering new business suits you. Whether you decide you're ready to grab a megaphone or remain on the sidelines a little bit longer, we aim to make this an easy and enjoyable training session.

CHAPTER 1

What Media Exposure Can Do for You—and What It Can't!

Before media cutbacks, it was common for editors across the country to require business reporters to write a little feature story about an interesting small company. When reporters seek out subjects for news stories like these, those select businesses become lucky winners of the media jackpot.

Lucky, in fact, can be an understatement. Executives and entrepreneurs dream about a positive mention in the media for numerous reasons: to gain greater recognition among existing customers, neighbors and suppliers; to realize a spike in sales; to promote a healthy community image that can please regulatory boards; to end a dispute with neighbors on good terms; to garner instant respect when meeting new people; or to tell the public of important news that may impact their world.

Most executives, however, believe that they'd have to commit a crime in order to merit a story. For many businesses, favorable coverage in the press seems nearly impossible. If convinced they have a worthy story, many don't know where to take their news. Upon locating the appropriate person, they wonder what to say to reporters, who have a frustrating way of putting people on the spot. Urged to be quick about their pitch or call back, those who are not accustomed to dealing with media types feel like they're wasting time and give up.

But before giving up, you should first realize that journalism, like every other industry, has its drivers and dynamics. Taking time to understand the industry can significantly improve the odds of a successful interaction and, in turn, yield a generous payoff.

Without question, having the community think favorably about your business is beneficial, and the public often sees a news story as a third-party endorsement. Friends and associates also acquire a different view of an organization that enjoys positive media exposure. And an internal ego boost is unbeatable. Though hard to quantify, the recognition enjoyed by personnel at all levels can come in handy. In addition to building morale and confidence, a nod just might open doors.

Ed Van Herik

Before major media cutbacks, I wrote a story for the Los Angeles Daily News on a small LA whitewater rafting company that ran trips on the Kern River in Central California. I surprised the owner, who did not expect to hear from a reporter, when I contacted him for background information. Having started the business as a sideline, he had never worked with the media but was able to pull together the information needed for the story and supply enthusiastic comments from his clients. Within two weeks after the story ran in the paper, the company posted a 40 percent spike in sales. While a big company often won't see such a change, a large sales boost sometimes happens to small commercial operations.

- When salespeople make cold calls, their reception will likely be a little warmer following a good news story that gave prospective customers a preliminary introduction.

- Cultivating good will within the community through media coverage of positive initiatives can pave the way if, for example, new permits are needed or attract quality talent if the organization is ready to expand.

- The right exposure can help nonprofits tee up donations when fundraising.

Even so, let's be clear about what to expect from public relations in general and media relations in particular: Positive press does not necessarily yield a one-to-one correlation at the cash register. While the gains can be multifold, no guarantee exists. Additionally, efforts to garner positive press can sometimes fall flat because, unlike a communication that is predetermined for a paid advertisement, the message that results through media relations is not a sure thing.

Likewise, appearing on the front page isn't always a blessing. Media coverage has a downside, one that is most apparent during a crisis. Consider the ramifications of a product recall or a CEO's personal breakdown. We all know how quick and merciless the press can be. Regrettably, many businesses fumble during the initial steps of a crisis and then spend years trying to recover. Some never recuperate from a media disaster, which is why cheerleaders who shift the crowd's focus are so highly valued. (We'll discuss this topic in Chapter 11.)

If public relations now seems more daunting than ever to you, consider the idea of pitching to the media in terms of pitching a product you know well. Once you grasp the dynamics of the transaction, if not all the specifics, you'll understand how to reach out to the media as you would to your target market. After all, working with the media is a type of business transaction, one in which information, not money, is the medium of exchange. You give the news. The reporter gets the story. You gain the press.

Key Points:

- Media relations can offer heightened awareness opportunities, but not necessarily one-to-one sales results.

- An organization can use positive press to boost its presence in the community.

- An organization can use the press to heighten awareness of a preplanned event.

CHAPTER 2

The Media: Looking at the Big Picture

We are bombarded *relentlessly*, most would agree, by emails, tweets, instant messages, pop-up ads, radio, TV, billboards, promotional items and more. All things considered, would you be surprised to learn that the average American sees at least 3,000 advertisements, logos, labels and news stories in a 24-hour period?

Asked to buy or give something by more sources than we could ever name, we filter information, consciously and subconsciously. Our ability to delete, block and ignore messages poses opportunities and challenges for organizations that aim to slip their communications past the barriers.

The big opportunity: Target audiences (often potential clients) tend to sort messages by concentrating on a handful of information outlets. Therefore, by putting their insights about audiences' habits to work, decision makers can potentially reach their specifically targeted groups at lower costs and with less effort than in previous years.

The primary challenge: To reach their targets, enterprises and nonprofits must figure out where their audiences go for news.

The confusion begins with the sheer number of communications channels. Network television, once

Ed Van Herik

Sometimes, you can secure coverage for your organization by hooking into an existing story. Once, while attending an event to unveil the latest electric cars that had just arrived at a dealership, I found a way to get several TV interviews for my utility employer—suggesting that viewers would naturally have questions about charging the vehicles. The TV reporters agreed, I did the interviews, and the utility got several positive mentions in a story that really wasn't theirs to begin with.

the only TV option, operates along with countless cable stations and Internet sites like Hulu. Similarly, not so long ago, we had only AM and FM radio stations that could reach listeners within limited ranges. Currently, satellite radio and podcasts provide a tailored listening experience for commuters stuck in their cars. Similarly, daily newspapers, once the dominant sources of news in large cities, must woo subscribers and occasional readers while countless print and online contenders compete for the same audiences.

At one time, media relations experts effectively blanketed the market when they got their stories in the daily newspaper and on TV. Today, the abundance of options and the need to zero in on key information channels used by target audiences have turned media research into an in-depth process.

The work begins by matching the topic and message to a list of media outlets and reporters who might be receptive. Again, an organization might have multiple messages that vary over time and by audience. Therefore, determining the most beneficial media outlets to reach a particular audience requires a savvy, realistic perspective. A spot on the 11 o'clock news, for instance, might be an ego boost for a local restaurant owner, but a favorable write-up in the local free publication might generate more new business—more quickly—for substantially less effort and cost. And a B-to-B company might gain more traction from an article in a trade publication than a TV appearance.

The proliferation of news outlets inspires many PR professionals to line up a mix of appropriate communications channels. Recognizing the value of reaching all pertinent audiences in an expanded media market, they understand that no single formula—or single media outlet—will deliver optimal results for every client.

Furthermore, message clarity is essential. The pitch—the explanation of why a media outlet would be interested in a specific business or nonprofit—remains a game changer. Ideally, the proposal will be a crisp, well-rehearsed message delivered so compellingly that a neutral journalist will decide to write about it.

Once clear about the messaging and targeted recipients, today's PR professional begins the work of designing an outreach proposal to reach prospective audiences through multiple channels.

Key Points:

- Today's organizations need to pinpoint which media sources their target audiences use.

- The most obvious choices are not always the optimal media options for certain target groups and particular messages.

- Utilizing multiple media channels enables organizations to ensure they're reaching their target audience, no matter where they get their news.

- The pitch can change the game.

CHAPTER 3

Today's Media: What's Out There?

An overview of today's media outlets must include longstanding resources like city newspapers, as well as a host of new channels created by technological innovation. The reasons for placing news in one type of vehicle (such as print or online) or in certain publications versus others are not always apparent. Good decisions come from evaluating the differences among the categories and components.

Let's take a look at the major outlets that need to be considered in any campaign.

Newspapers

Remember leather helmets, Howard Cosell, the flying wedge? If you haven't yet seen your first grey hair or don't see yourself as a sports history buff, you might be unfamiliar with football relics that, although hardly mentioned today, were 20th century staples. At one time, nearly everyone knew Howard Cosell was *the* announcer for NFL Monday Night Football.

Similarly, once a staple in every household, the print edition of the daily newspaper is quickly becoming a media relic. Formerly the primary source of news, behemoth newspapers are even shying away from making endorsements so they don't risk alienating any of their readers. It's just a fact that newspapers today struggle to keep pace with Internet entrepreneurs and niche publications. Many have failed, and those that strive to remain in the game are reevaluating their business models.

The big papers' efforts to compete include everything from revamping formats to implementing new products. Special interest sections—business news, for example—present opportunities for well-timed reports on the latest happenings, perhaps a retailer's expansion or a nonprofit's recently added service. Similarly, zoned editions, or segments of papers that reach certain neighborhoods and outlying communities, tend to serve companies that have pertinent news for those regions. Businesses located within the zone and/or are generating news within the zone generally have the best chances for media coverage by the local reporters assigned to cover such areas.

In addition to the zoned sections of larger papers, independent publications are moving into many small towns and neighborhoods. Usually offered to the public for free and distributed on a weekly basis, locally focused papers tend to generate the bulk of their revenue from advertisements. Whether or not they advertise, companies seeking local coverage are likely to have greater success upon making a solid, hyper-local pitch to a neighborhood newspaper than to the zoned section of a major metro newspaper.

When weighing the pros and cons, avoid the mistake of equating *neighborhood* to *amateur*. Neighborhood newspaper chains can be huge. For example, the Neighbor Newspapers, which cover many Atlanta area communities, claim a total circulation of around 900,000. By contrast, Atlanta's major daily newspaper, the *Atlanta Journal-Constitution*, distributes more than 231,000 copies daily and over 644,000 Sunday editions. A story in the *Atlanta Journal-Constitution* will reach all of those 231,000 readers. Yet an article in a neighborhood publication—even if it is part of a larger chain—may only reach one small area, versus sometimes reaching the chain's total audience.

Local Niche Publications

A variety of niche publications exist in most urban areas. Popular types include a business weekly, an arts publication, an alternative weekly, and a parenting magazine. Editors and reporters from each tend to be receptive to story ideas from organizations that are involved in their areas of interest.

Radio

Radio stations once controlled the field, especially in large, urban areas. While trapped in their cars, coming and going each day, commuters relied on their local and syndicated shows for company. Drivers still tune into their local radio stations for traffic information and attention-grabbing news stories, but podcasts and satellite radio now give captive audiences a greater range of options. However, local radio programs, including all-news stations, should not be overlooked; they remain hungry for fresh content, and opportunities exist for those who are nimble. Hosts of specialty programs throughout most major markets additionally offer on-air interview time to nonprofits and businesses. Radio tours are often put together by a PR professional pitching a story to relevant radio stations, and building blocks of interview times on specific dates. This works best if you have an articulate, possibly well-known, spokesperson and a hot topic.

TV

Television news hasn't lost its punch, even as the rest of the media market morphs around it. Producing television news is relatively cheap, so the abundance of local and national programs presents numerous opportunities for organizations to pitch unique stories. Also, include local and national television guest spots on your list of possibilities to consider. Producers and hosts are continually on the lookout for interesting interviews. To prepare, keep in mind that visuals are essential for television, and a broadly appealing storyline is preferable. Sometimes a well-known celebrity spokesperson, who agrees to be available for a few hours for interviews, is booked on a television satellite tour. Then, the PR people line up interviews with stations throughout the targeted geographic area, one after another. Specialty PR firms are generally hired because they know the technical details needed to meld interviews with news outlets, and they have the established media contacts needed to make the tours a success.

Internet News Organizations

The Internet has spawned a number of online news organizations that cater to local communities. For instance, Patch.com, the brainchild of AOL, consists of hyper-local news sites in communities around the country. Other online-only sources—Slate.com, for example—will tackle broader topics.

Most major newspapers, attempting to capitalize on the Internet, have created small online newsrooms that post breaking news throughout the day. The *Christian Science Monitor* and *U.S. News & World Report,* once printed publications, folded the paper versions but have a strong online presence. In some instances, an organization's story will migrate from a mainline paper's printed publication to the online version, or vice versa. Other features achieve only online or print exposure.

Magazines

Thousands of magazines—industry trade, niche consumer, political news—comprise the media landscape. In addition to allowing an organization to feature news in an in-depth format, they also provide space for professional spotlights that include photography and highlight personnel, endeavors, products and other important matters. Some are pegged to a particular industry, such as heating and air conditioning or church facilities, while others are defined by broader category topics like beauty or dining. While a number of magazines have folded over the past decade, subscribers have held onto certain beloved, must-read publications, leaving plenty of opportunity for newsmakers.

Social Media

While often considered a separate publicity tactic, social media overlaps media relations so much that many PR professionals now evaluate the two areas together. Social media, in fact, provides informal avenues for meeting reporters, since many of them, who can be hard to reach on the phone or through email, are active on Twitter, Facebook and LinkedIn. On top of that, some reporters ask their followers for story ideas on Twitter and Facebook. In this case, social media is simply a new format through which a media relations professional can make a pitch.

Once a story runs, an organization can extend its reach considerably by posting links to the feature on their social media sites. Importantly, PR professionals monitor social media activity to ensure that news flows among traditional and social media channels. (The next chapter addresses other considerations.)

Ed Van Herik

Just like a pitcher needs to know a batter's strengths and weaknesses to get a strike, a media relations practitioner needs to know where a client's pitch will find the greatest success among the wealth of media outlets currently available. For example, to overcome a popular concern that electric vehicles (EVs) could not cover the distance on a charge that most gas-powered cars could travel on a tank of gas, the local utility in San Diego joined with Costco, Saturn, a local mall and a hospital chain to demonstrate how easy EVs are to recharge. Catering to TV's lust for visuals, they ran a caravan of EVs around the county, stopping at popular locations with charging stations. The event, designed for TV with good visuals and an easy-to-follow storyline, received more than 20 broadcast mentions within two days.

Debbie Graham Fitzgerald

One of my clients, a pet expert, had a broad audience: those who love pets. But there was more to his story because he was an animal communicator—he talked to animals! Many would question the validity of a guy who claimed to talk to animals, so I knew I was taking a risk in exposing him to skeptics. My first outreach, nevertheless, was to a carefully selected Associated Press reporter. (AP, which is a not-for-profit news cooperative owned by American newspapers and broadcast members, supplies news to members and subscribers worldwide.) I figured if I was going to reach a large audience, AP would be a good choice of media to target. The initial pitch was positive, and soon after I was setting up an interview that the AP reporter conducted by phone from her New York City apartment. Her misbehaving cats were beside her, so she had the animal communicator talk to the felines over the phone. Remarkably, she reported that her cats behaved better afterwards because of the expert's interaction with them! The result: A feature story about my client and his expertise was published in print and online across the nation. On top of that, one day after the article was published, a producer from a popular talk show taped in New York City offered to fly him up to be a guest on the show. We both got a flight and a night's stay in Times Square. Even better, the exposure garnered new clients—from Oregon to England—for this now well-exposed pet expert. The case is the perfect example of a media snowball.

Key Points:

- Decision makers should be familiar with their media options to discern which are best suited to the organization and why.

- Local media—radio, TV, specialized print publications, online sites—are accessible to organizations and they reach valuable audiences.

- Social media networks, including Twitter, Facebook and LinkedIn, provide backdoor access to journalists who are swamped with emails and phone calls.

CHAPTER 4

Social Media and Related Avenues: What They Offer—and Don't

Social media are a lot like the kids on the baseball team in *The Bad News Bears* movies. Scrappy and a bit rough, they have a hard time convincing people they belong in the game—despite obvious victories.

Likewise, many organizations with pertinent news to share continue to wonder: *Should we enter the social media game?* To answer, see if you can say *yes* to the following questions:

- Will social media enhance your communications with a particular audience?

- Will the individual platform(s) under consideration boost your organization's reputation?
- Will social media allow your organization to gain a clearer understanding of what customers think about your product or service?

If your responses are positive at this point, can you also say that your organization has the budget, time and resources to manage social media successfully? Are you prepared to develop and follow a strategic plan? If so, the effort is worth pursuing.

Caution: Don't just jump in. Find out how social media will help you and set some goals.

Before proceeding, let's pause to consider the role of media relations in social media. Some view the social media realm as a completely separate PR tactic, but media relations and social media go hand in hand, for several reasons:

First, various social media are among all other tools that a PR practitioner can use to disseminate a message. Whether pitching to a blogger or adding content to a social media site, the person holding the megaphone for any organization should coordinate each message to ensure consistency and relevance.

Second, social media is relevant to journalists, who scan social media sites to enhance their reporting. More than 80 percent of journalists polled in December 2011 by Zoomerang, an online survey tool, used social media channels to search for story ideas. In fact, we have seen entire news hours devoted to what's trending on social media.

Third, most traditional media outlets have an online component that allows readers or viewers to "share" via numerous social media channels like Facebook, Twitter, Digg, etc. Sharing with social media audiences increases the PR impressions gained from traditional media outlets.

Still, social media is not free. Someone must set up social media accounts and keep them current and updated with thoughtful messaging. Whether you fill the position with an employee or outsource the work to an independent PR counselor, you'll need an ongoing budget for those services.

Engaging in social media sometimes comes with limitations. Most firms in the financial industry, for instance, operate under the microscope of regulators. Compliance officers either forbid online interactions or require a review of every post, creating a burdensome task for a high-paid employee. Considering the potential risk of being fined, some firms post only the most basic, company-approved information.

Additionally, social media can backfire, as when audiences react negatively to a posted message. Words alone have catapulted many organizations into a crisis communication mode, so those who tweet and post should know that celebrities are not the only ones who can land on the defensive.

Bottom line: Think before leaping into social media. Determine what kinds of controls are necessary and who will take responsibility for your program. At a minimum, consider establishing a social media policy. Employees need guidelines about what they can say online regarding employer matters. Beyond establishing rules, many organizations implement monitoring systems to prevent rogue employees from misbehaving, as in sharing company secrets.

If you don't have a budget or time to engage with social media properly, consider setting up a few accounts on popular sites (LinkedIn, Twitter and Facebook) to post good news from time to time and call it a day. Search engines will find your posts, and that's always positive.

Debbie Graham Fitzgerald

A number of sports involve playing with a ball, but the rules of engagement differ widely. Similarly, while considered a tool of public relations, social media comes with an entirely different set of ground rules. Beyond understanding the intricacies of various media, players must pay attention to the rapidly changing field and be ready to shift strategies and tactics to score.

Key Points:

- Decision makers should understand the role social media plays in the PR mix and determine which social media are appropriate in light of the organization's objectives.

- Social media is not only relevant to journalists but also interfaces with traditional media outlets.

- The organization's messages should be consistent among all social media.

- Social media messages should adhere to professional/industry compliance requirements.

- Social media efforts are neither cost-free nor risk-free.

CHAPTER 5

Preparing to Enter the Media Relations Game: The Nuts and Bolts

Question: Why should a company spokesperson think like a reporter?

Answer: It is easier to make connections with people if you are already speaking their language.

Given the fierce competition for media attention, seeing your organization through the eyes of the media will help empower your head cheerleader to promote your organization, energize old fans and win new ones, and inspire those contacts to do their part in fueling your entity's success.

Tactic No. 1: Research the media market, the competition and the industry.

No organization exists in a vacuum. It has relationships with neighbors, clients, vendors and other types of organizations, including competitors. All those relationships will shape a company's outreach and need to be considered before deciding what types of news will draw the attention of reporters.

It is common for PR practitioners to research both competitors and pertinent media outlets and reporters as part of the initial planning for a media campaign to determine which reporters are most likely to be receptive. In addition, the research will usually include a broad review of key trends in a client's industry so that any major successes or incidents can be accounted for in planning.

Tactic No. 2: See your business or nonprofit the way the media does.

Imagine, for a moment, the duties of a daily newspaper reporter on an active beat. Getting an early start at work, the reporter trudges through 100 or more email and voicemail pitches. Skimming and deleting one message after another, the journalist finds one that stands out.

What's different about that *one*? Two critical components will catch a reporter's attention: 1) pertinent news, and 2) a sufficiently solid and credible source to pique interest and inform readers.

To evaluate whether or not you have attention-grabbing news, you'll want to adopt the critical view of a seasoned journalist. Two areas should fall under your scrutiny: 1) the merits of your news, and 2) the qualifications of those who will speak for your organization.

News and Spokesperson Considerations:

- *Who would care about the news? Why would they care?*

  If, for example, a company is adding a new location with 100 new jobs, the news would interest elected officials who could expect additional tax revenues; vendors that would supply products and services; restaurant owners and other retailers in the vicinity; utilities that would supply power, and others.

- *Is the company's news newsworthy? Why?*

  The news regarding the business expansion above indicates that 100 people in the area would find jobs, or that 100 people would be relocating to the area. Either of those economic developments would affect city operations, incurring city costs, which could impact taxes. And for people out of work, the news is something they can use.

- *Is the news unique? If so, can you prove the matter's distinctiveness?*

  Falling within the category of unique news would be to accomplish something that research shows no other organization in your industry, region, state or city has done. In some cases, it can be considered unique if no one in your region has done it.

- *Does the story relate to your organization's expertise— the defined topic(s) about which your experts can inform and educate an audience?*

  If you are in the mortgage business, for instance, and the government wants to tighten regulatory control, your comments will be welcome in the newsroom— if your perspective is fresh and your spokesperson is articulate.

- *Who will be the organization's spokesperson(s)?*

  A company spokesperson is almost always automatically considered an expert in that individual's industry.

  (Read more about choosing a spokesperson in Chapter 6.)

Tactic No. 3: Communicate with the media before sending a press release.

Having the right contacts in the media from which to build a solid media database is fundamental to garnering successful publicity. Begin with a well-defined target audience to ensure that you target journalists who reach your desired contacts.

Media relations professionals either already know key reporters or target them by accessing subscription-based databases. Up-to-date records deliver a wealth of information about members of the media, including their contact information, ways they do and do not like to be pitched, their publications' circulation numbers, and much more. Lacking a useful database, you might as well jump into a new game without the proper equipment or knowing the rules about how to play.

Once the target list of reporters is assembled, carefully plan your first media interaction. Realize that most reporters are neutral when they initially hear from a company. Even those who have heard of you or your organization don't typically have preconceived notions.

While we commonly hear complaints about media bias, it is a mistake to assume that any one reporter has an axe to grind, especially if you've never dealt with her or him. Some outlets concentrate on simply putting out the most informative story possible, given their time constraints. Others do have a point of view. Part of your initial research should uncover any potential bias, allowing a company or nonprofit to plan accordingly.

To make a positive first impression, approach the media with the following considerations:

- Communicate to the appropriate media representative.

- Aim to intrigue the individual with a well-planned pitch.

- Gauge his or her interest as you speak.

- Be mindful of the media contact's time.

- Don't engage in a hard sell.
- Don't stalk the media contact.

The media pitch is not a sales pitch, and the purpose of media relations is not to create a marketing piece. Maintaining a knowledgeable, helpful tone, the professional operates with the mindset of providing information. Selling—telling everyone how great the company is—should not be on the agenda. Also, the spokesperson who achieves the most success with media is truthful and transparent, as well as respectful of the journalist's time.

Expect relatively quick exchanges when contacting journalists. Most reporters know immediately if a topic fits within their bailiwick. Those who aren't sure tend to ask a few qualifying questions, but when journalists are not interested, the professional takes no for an answer. There's always another pitch, so don't burn a bridge from overzealousness. Without pressing the issue, however, you might ask your contact if he or she can suggest someone else in the newsroom who would be interested in the story idea.

Tactic No. 4: Know when to write a press release ... and when not to!

Contrary to what some social media gurus say, the press release is alive and well. A great tool to help build an organization's main messages, a press release covers who, what, when, where, why and how—the basics learned in elementary school.

Ed Van Herik

Persistence counts, if applied intelligently. Early in my career, I put on a local media event in Los Angeles to unveil an array of solar power projects. The event was a dud; one reporter came and even he didn't bother writing about it. I chose one of the projects, however, to repackage for TV with a new pitch on how the technology would be useful in the Third World. Both CNN and a syndicated technology show, which went into more than 80 countries, picked it up, broadcasting the feature worldwide. The story would be the best single media hit the company had that year.

Why bother writing a release?

First, the vehicle provides the "full skinny" about an organization's news in one place. Most reporters are also familiar with the format, so the piece is an easy go-to place for information.

Second, a press release is a terrific leveraging tool. A company can post the piece online, either to selected media outlets or on the organization's website; send the write-up to clients and stakeholders in an email; or distribute the release via wire services.

Third, a well-written press release is often published—with or without edits—directly into targeted media.

Some announcements call for a press release:

- New products or services

- Deal completions

- New hires and promotions

- Mergers and acquisitions

- Events

- Awards or achievement recognition

- Speaking engagements

- Charitable contributions

We'll cover the press release format in the next chapter, but for the time being, let's focus on when and when not to write a press release.

When should you *not* write a press release? The simple answer: No news is *no news*.

In other words, write a release only when you have news to share. Adhering to the rule is especially important when building relationships with media people. Reading one press release after another that offers no news is so grueling that some reporters retaliate by posting "bad pitches" on their blogs. *Ouch.* One of the fastest ways for a media spokesperson to acquire an unprofessional reputation is to waste reporters' time.

In the spirit of respecting others' time by sharing only newsworthy information, present your news without wasting words. To convey all pertinent facts, including background notes and quotes, some press releases read like short articles. In other cases, a brief yet informative text or tweet with a link to a website is sufficient to intrigue the media contact and convey the point. The reporter will call the organization's spokesperson for details.

Ed Van Herik

At times, a quick text or tweet will draw interest, especially if the topic is related to developing news. For instance, during a cold snap or a heat wave, this text or tweet would likely be read carefully by a reporter.

Here's an example of a text pitch:

"My client installs geothermal HVAC systems, which heat and cool a home for a tiny fraction of a homeowner's current bill. That's a big plus this season."

A tweet pitch would look like this:

"Geothermal systems now being installed to slash seasonal energy bills. (Link to more information.)"

Tactic No. 5: Think outside the press release to generate news.

How often does your organization generate meaningful news? Now that you possibly have a clearer sense of your megaphone's value and purpose, do you find that you produce more or less legitimate news than you originally thought? Are your events ongoing or cyclical?

Businesses often find themselves in "no-news" periods—and that's OK. Media relations are not only about promoting an organization's news; the

Ed Van Herik

A utility in the Southwest would regularly give a briefing in early June about the state of the electricity supply for the area as they headed into the hot summer season. Because the region had been affected by blackouts, major media always made a point of attending the sessions.

Typical, ongoing events for the utility would entail news regarding corporate earnings reports, introduction of new products, reminders about bills and sales, and tips on how to best use products already purchased.

responsibilities are also about sharing knowledge and expertise with members of the media and, ultimately, the audiences they reach.

Utilize no-news periods as opportunities to build a rapport with reporters, editors and producers while keeping your business or nonprofit in the news. One tactic is to scour current news stories upon which your spokesperson can comment. When a journalist does a story on conditions in your industry, for instance, call the person on the day the story runs, praise the article and offer to give more insight.

Don't expect a story resulting from your interaction to materialize the next day; that only happens sometimes. Instead, take the view that you're building a relationship

Debbie Graham Fitzgerald

Pitching during no-news periods can be exhilarating. One morning, I reached out to about ten reporters who covered my client's beat (banking). I had previously built a rapport with those media contacts on my client's behalf. Reminding them about my client's expertise, I asked if such expert thoughts would be useful on any of the stories they were working on. By the end of the day, I had two interviews set up! Yes, I was doing my happy dance!

that will pay off later. Success is more probable if the reporter covers the field regularly.

Before reaching out, spend some time reading the reporter's other stories found on the same publication's website or in other sources. A journalist is usually flattered to learn that an industry expert is following his or her work. At the same time, your research can reveal what and how the journalist likes to cover his or her beat—observations that will help you pitch stories.

With a little planning, you (or your spokesperson) can become the reporter's go-to expert. Though

Ed Van Herik

An economic development corporation in Southern California had one executive who knew exactly how to garner publicity as an expert. A top economist, the individual was quoted in story after story, in print and on the air, about every aspect of local business. He was known among reporters to give a nearly instant assessment about any plant closing, opening, construction trend, transportation proposal or new invention. As a reporter, I wryly asked him if he dreamed up a different quote for each reporter. "I try to," he answered seriously.

knowledgeable about their specialized areas, journalists do not have the same insights that come from working directly in an industry every day. As a result, certain elements, like evolving trends, are important to verify from industry insiders before journalists decide whether to write their articles. Reporters also look to the same sources for short, simple explanations or assessments that they can relay to audiences. Consequently, your expertise can be appreciated behind the scenes as well as noted to readers.

Tactic No. 6: Consider media training.

If an executive has not worked with reporters in the past, or if the individual has experience but is out of practice, attempting a media interview without a briefing can be daunting. That's where media training comes in.

Many PR media relations professionals offer seminars—usually conducted over several hours in one day—on how to deal with the media. The pro typically gives an overview of the media market, describes how reporters approach stories, and explains how to craft succinct answers to typical questions. Executives also learn how to segue from a reporter's negative observation or question to positive talking points. Additionally, most sessions entail mock interviews that place executives in front of the camera for review. Such exercises effectively get key personnel into the media relations mindset.

Debbie Graham Fitzgerald

We PR folks realize that "perfection" in delivering a message doesn't always happen overnight. Likewise, while in media training, make sure you open your mind to being a person who can be directed as well as one who will accept constructive criticism. In fact, I listen in on calls with clients and media in order to provide prompt, straightforward feedback.

When listening in on one client spokesperson who needed continuous coaching on brevity, I kept wondering when he'd pause. His response—a four-paragraph answer—droned on for minutes. Finally, I jumped in to ask, "Hey reporter, you still there?" Indeed, the reporter was no longer on the line. We'd accidentally been disconnected for some time! Before we reconnected, I took the opportunity to coach the client to remember to pause every now and then and, perhaps, to ask the reporter if the question was answered and whether his explanation was clear.

Tactic No. 7: Prepare for the pitch.

Explaining to journalists why they should cover an organization is a little like describing professional baseball to people watching a game for the first time. To cover the compelling points without overwhelming your media contact, your description should be condensed, complete, and easy to understand—all practical criteria since journalists don't have much time to consider any single pitch coming in cold.

Today's downsized news organizations expect journalists to cover more stories across more media platforms. Consequently, reporters, squeezed to meet deadlines, often draft one story for several outlets. Recently, a reporter of Atlanta's NPR station completed a radio segment about giving to The Salvation Army. She then filed and posted her entire interview online as well as tweeted on Twitter.

Since journalists must typically accomplish more in less time, you must quickly and convincingly explain why a story promises to engage readers and viewers. Be prepared. Clarify your organization's message prior to reaching out to the media.

To develop your key points, pay attention to the notable comments and quotes that you come across in the daily news. You might be surprised that TV quotes typically range from five to ten seconds—that's all. Similarly, unless an article features a particular individual, the average quote from any one person in a print story is seldom more than 15 words. Therefore, to prepare your presentation, draft a declarative sentence of eight to 15 words apiece for each fact you intend to present.

By keeping your remarks brief, you'll maximize your chance to be quoted rather than paraphrased.

Finally, determine the three most important facts that the reporter should learn from you. That's your pitch.

Fight the temptation to volunteer excessive details. Instead of improving your odds for a favorable story, a glut of information confuses the issue. A reporter could end up telling a story that interests audiences but misses the point that your organization aimed to make.

Ed Van Herik

When the National Academy of Sciences issued a release debunking the assertion that electromagnetic fields (EMF) were responsible for cancer, TV reporters went to the local utility, which had been involved in court battles over the issue. After agreeing to use three key talking points, the company's expert let loose a torrent of technical information that left the reporter dazed—and the story confused.

Key Points:

- Contact the media with legitimate news or the ability to offer expert commentary.

- Thoroughly prepare your organization's media spokesperson.

- Know when to write a press release.

- Develop each pitch to the media from a journalist's point of view and with your organization's strategy in mind.

CHAPTER 6

The Spokesperson: Your Business' Champion

Several key items should come into play when you pick the ideal spokesperson for your team. Without question, the individual should be presentable and neat, and someone to whom ordinary people can relate.

To screen for the right person, consider the following:

- The spokesperson needs to speak in complete sentences and stop when the point is made. While a spokesperson is presenting the company's point of view, a media interview is not a sales job, so talking more isn't going to persuade the reporter. Also, only one or two quotes will be used in the story. By sticking to three main talking points, your spokesperson increases the odds that one or two of them will be used. Say too much, and the story wanders.

- The person needs to be unflappable. Reporters will ask tough questions, and a spokesperson who starts sputtering isn't going to convey the image of an in-control company.

- The spokesperson needs to dress appropriately. Business attire and neat casual clothes will generally create a decent impression. Large, jangling earrings and tight, patterned clothing can create visual distractions when a spokesperson is trying to make a point. In addition to simple patterns, blue used to be recommended because the color showed up well on TV. While high-definition TV makes the choice of blue less of a necessity, styles and colors should enable viewers to concentrate on the message, not the spokesperson's apparel.

- The person needs to be teachable. An individual's expertise in a field doesn't automatically make a company spokesperson an expert in media relations. Media relations is a highly stylized interaction, different from other business encounters, and a spokesperson must have the ability to take direction that will ensure the company delivers the optimal information in the best possible light. The ideal spokesperson needs to be more of a conduit than a content creator.

- The spokesperson should be relatively free of media bias. Questioning the objectivity of journalists is currently fashionable, but whether or not a reporter has any biases on a particular subject, bringing an attitude into an interview simply increases the chances for a poor story. A spokesperson needs to present the organization in a positive or, at least, a thoughtful light.

- Some research suggests that viewers trust attractive spokespersons more readily, but determining exactly how to use that insight is difficult. Mannerisms, an overall helpful approach, and a face with character can be just as appealing.

While it is tempting to ask the CEO to be the company spokesperson, that person might not be the optimal choice. To begin, the spokesperson needs to accessible, and many top executives are booked solid with meetings. Also, some CEOs are true believers in their company, and they find it difficult to respond to skeptical questions with equanimity. A spokesperson needs to be available, articulate, relatively calm, and knowledgeable—to a point.

As a matter of fact, if the spokesperson is not a top executive, then reporters will not expect them to have all the answers to their questions on the spot. So, if a difficult question is asked, the spokesperson can delay responding until a good answer is crafted.

One tactic that your company may want to explore is to offer up a spokesperson from your organization

Ed Van Herik

At the beginning of the California Energy Crisis, I was working as a media relations manager at San Diego Gas & Electric, the epicenter of the crisis. At first, the company put forth a vice president to respond to media inquiries, but it quickly became apparent that the executive was left doing nothing else but answering the avalanche of daily requests.

When I became the principle TV spokesman, the VP could return to her primary job and the company could devote adequate attention to media requests. I handled four or five interviews a day during the week and sometimes a couple on the weekends, providing media with a reliable channel to receive the company's input into breaking stories.

The company also benefitted because I was not an officer; I could say that I didn't immediately know the answer to tough questions and my response was believable. That gave us more time to craft a better response than an off-the-cuff reply, which always presents a danger, especially for an executive who is expected to know the answer.

to serve as an expert source on key topics. Such a spokesperson ideally should be a good extemporaneous speaker, one who is both credible and coachable. Once chosen, a spokesperson (possibly you) becomes the voice of the organization, so the individual must stay on point at all times. Internal interviews, which help prepare a spokesperson, should pose a variety of questions, including those that seem off-the-wall.

Not surprisingly, training is also a vetting process. Not every expert is the best candidate to speak on your organization's behalf.

Upon determining and preparing your spokesperson with topics and talking points, proceed to contacting reporters, coordinating introductions and offering a brief list of topics. (You can send a press release at a later time.)

Key Points:

- Take some time to screen for the right spokesperson. Remember, they will be representing your organization during a high-profile period.

- The best spokesperson is not necessarily the CEO. Working with the media can be time-consuming, and their time might be better spent handling the overall crisis.

CHAPTER 7

The Tools: Be Properly Equipped

The Press Release

A press release is nothing more than a stylized, capsule report on what an organization or entrepreneur believes is news. Components include a compelling headline, a zippy lead paragraph that elaborates on the headline, backup quotes and other information, and a contact person's phone number and email. Written a little like a news story, a press release delivers the most important information first and concludes with a short description of the company or organization.

The headline—written to "tell and sell"—should be short, snappy and, above all, accurate. The headline intends to pull in readers, so the body of the release should follow through, backing up any initial claims.

The lead paragraph must answer the five questions that most news stories ask: *who, what, where, when* and *how.* Take time to make your lead paragraph exciting yet scrupulously accurate and information-filled.

Quotes give the opportunity to plug the product or service shamelessly. If you want to tell your audience that your new product deserves a gold medal for innovation, quote individuals who can convincingly make the point on behalf of your organization.

Further information can elaborate on the value of the organization's product or service, as well as provide context regarding why the news is important.

The boilerplate, also the last paragraph, contains a standard description of the entity that appears in all releases. Facts can include the market area and customers you serve, where you are headquartered, and the problems solved by your products or services.

Contact information tells the journalist whom to call for more information. Since reporters generally regard a press release as the start of the story, most journalists, but not all, follow up for details. The contact person, therefore, must be readily available over the first few days after the release goes out. Often, the president insists on being the primary contact, but organizations should avoid the mistake of naming an executive who will be tied up in meetings or otherwise inaccessible for comments. The spokesperson must be someone who can and will be responsive.

The finished news release should have 300 to 500 words, tops. Phrase the content simply and get to the point quickly. The temptation to outline every detail, racking up 800 to 1,000 words, can be strong, especially when an overly enthusiastic CEO has a strong say. Therefore, keep in mind that reporters who receive 25 or more releases daily are more tempted to delete than read a long-winded write-up. The general rule: one idea, one release.

For this book, we wanted to offer an example of a press release. During the writing process, we decided to each write our own and present it to each other. The exercise was a fun experiment, and the challenge enabled us to hit upon an important lesson: Two PR pros might take two entirely different approaches when writing a press release, but both can be winners if the pieces are well-written and contain all the pertinent information.

New Book Reveals the Secrets of Achieving Media Relations Success
Publicity-Expert Authors Share Insider Tips for Developing Effective Publicity Campaigns

ATLANTA, February XX, 2014 — Thanks to a pair of Atlanta-area public relations (PR) experts, the secrets of media relations success are now accessible to business leaders everywhere. Their newly released book, *Megaphones Be With You*, is a matter-of-fact, behind-the-scenes peek at the intricacies of promoting a business and garnering publicity. Like a megaphone that amplifies a single voice, the book was written to educate CEOs, business owners, and corporate and nonprofit executives about how to reach greater numbers of people with their key messages—and provide these leaders with actionable strategies and tactics for doing so effectively.

Seasoned publicity pros Debbie Graham Fitzgerald and Ed Van Herik, each of whom owns a PR firm, collaborated on the book to share their expertise. The realm of media relations—orchestrating a cooperative communication effort with various media sources—can be challenging. "Many business leaders are knowledgeable about their industries and savvy about running their businesses, but often they have not figured out how to reach out to their target markets, much less gain any control over the message," said Van Herik, principal of Van Herik Communications.

Megaphones is meant to answer common questions about media relations that enterprise and nonprofit leaders have, such as:

- Where do I start?
- Will the strategy work for me?
- What can I do that I haven't been doing?
- Should I hire a professional?
- What's the cost and what's the return on investment?

To help their clients, the authors searched for books targeted to business professionals that explained how media relations works, but they did not find any that specifically addressed the art of media relations in a detailed way. So they decided to write their own book. "We find that we do a great deal of training and educating when we bring on new clients," said Fitzgerald, CEO of Fitzgerald PR Inc. "Media relations is often a misunderstood practice. We see it as the art of communicating news via people-focused distribution channels: targeted reporters, journalists, producers or bloggers. Also, the relations part of media relations is the key in cultivating the best opportunities to garner publicity. We achieve success when effective relationships are combined with powerful messaging that informs and captures the attention of the target audience."

Due to the comprehensive nature of *Megaphones*, Fitzgerald and Van Herik have dubbed it *The Best Media Relations Book Ever Written*—though in a tongue-in-cheek way. The authors share their extensive knowledge, honed through a combined 41 years in the PR industry, in the easy-to-read *Megaphones*. Readers can choose from an e-book available on Amazon.com and itunes.apple.com for $9.95, or a 154 page print-on-demand version for $12.95. *Megaphones* was edited by Sallie Boyles and designed by Henderson Shapiro Peck.

About the Authors

Debbie Graham Fitzgerald and Ed Van Herik have been friends and colleagues since 2009. They are both award-winning PR professionals who are active members of the Public Relations Society of America, Georgia chapter. Fitzgerald has been active in the PR field since 1995 and Van Herik since 1992. Prior to entering the PR industry, Debbie had a five-year marketing career in the entertainment business and Ed was a journalist for 20 years. Each specialize in the practice of media relations, and has garnered thousands of media interviews for clients in various industries throughout their careers. For more information, visit www.MegaphonesBeWithYou.com.

###

FOR IMMEDIATE RELEASE
PR Contact:
Debbie Graham Fitzgerald, Fitzgerald PR 770.887.6060

New Book Reveals the Secrets of Achieving Media Relations Success

Publicity-Expert Authors Share Insider Tips for Developing Effective Publicity Campaigns

ATLANTA, February XX, 2014 — Thanks to a pair of Atlanta-area public relations (PR) experts, the secrets of media relations success are now accessible to business leaders everywhere. Their newly released book, *Megaphones Be With You*, is a matter-of-fact, behind-the-scenes peek at the intricacies of promoting a business and garnering publicity. Like a megaphone that amplifies a single voice, the book was written to educate CEOs, business owners, and corporate and nonprofit executives about how to reach greater numbers of people with their key messages—and provide these leaders with actionable strategies and tactics for doing so effectively.

Seasoned publicity pros Debbie Graham Fitzgerald and Ed Van Herik, each of whom owns a PR firm, collaborated on the book to share their expertise. The realm of media relations—orchestrating a cooperative communication effort with various media sources—can be challenging. "Many business leaders are knowledgeable about their industries and savvy about running their businesses, but often they have not figured out how to reach out to their target markets, much less gain any control over the message," said Van Herik, principal of Van Herik Communications.

Megaphones is meant to answer common questions about media relations that enterprise and nonprofit leaders have, such as:

- Where do I start?
- Will the strategy work for me?
- What can I do that I haven't been doing?
- Should I hire a professional?
- What's the cost and what's the return on investment?

To help their clients, the authors searched for books targeted to business professionals that explained how media relations works, but they did not find any that specifically addressed the art of media relations in a detailed way. So they decided to write their own book. "We find that we do a great deal of training and educating when we bring on new clients," said Fitzgerald, CEO of Fitzgerald PR Inc. "Media relations is often a misunderstood practice. We see it as the art of communicating news via people-focused distribution channels: targeted reporters, journalists, producers or bloggers. Also, the relations part of media relations is the key in cultivating the best opportunities to garner publicity. We achieve success when effective relationships are combined with powerful messaging that informs and captures the attention of the target audience."

Due to the comprehensive nature of *Megaphones*, Fitzgerald and Van Herik have dubbed it *The Best Media Relations Book Ever Written*—though in a tongue-in-cheek way. The authors share their extensive knowledge, honed through a combined 41 years in the

PR industry, in the easy-to-read *Megaphones*. Readers can choose from an e-book available on Amazon.com and itunes.apple.com for $9.95, or a 154 page print-on-demand version for $12.95. *Megaphones* was edited by Sallie Boyles and designed by Henderson Shapiro Peck.

About the Authors

Debbie Graham Fitzgerald and Ed Van Herik have been friends and colleagues since 2009. They are both award-winning PR professionals who are active members of the Public Relations Society of America, Georgia chapter. Fitzgerald has been active in the PR field since 1995 and Van Herik since 1992. Prior to entering the PR industry, Debbie had a five-year marketing career in the entertainment business and Ed was a journalist for 20 years. Each specialize in the practice of media relations, and has garnered thousands of media interviews for clients in various industries throughout their careers. For more information, visit www.MegaphonesBeWithYou.com.

###

PR PROS UNVEIL GREATEST MEDIA RELATIONS BOOK EVER WRITTEN
Book Tells What Companies Need to Know to Work with Journalists

ATLANTA, February XX, 2014 — Veteran public relations professionals Ed Van Herik and Debbie Graham Fitzgerald have outlined what organizations need to know if they want to expand their business and avoid missteps in dealing with reporters and editors.

Written in an engaging style, their 154-page book, *Megaphones Be With You,* details how a company can decide if it has news, how to work with reporters, how to get coverage for a company or nonprofit even if they don't have news, and how to assess return on investment.

"Many businesses and nonprofits would like to boost their image through positive coverage, but they either don't know where to begin or they've tried and failed," said Debbie Graham Fitzgerald, CEO of Fitzgerald PR in Atlanta. "We lead them through the process of determining if a media relations program will be worthwhile and give them the information they need to develop a successful media campaign."

The book, nicknamed "The Greatest Media Relations Book Ever Written," uses an analytical approach, enlivened by real-life examples, to demonstrate:

- How to assess an organization's potential for getting media coverage;
- How to pick the appropriate media outlets and reporters;
- How to approach journalists effectively;
- How to leverage social media to maximize coverage;
- How to determine ROI.

"*Megaphones Be With You* describes how journalists look at their jobs, how to plug in to their existing mindset, and how to assess the various media opportunities available today," said Ed Van Herik, founder of Van Herik Communications in Atlanta. "This isn't rocket science, but it isn't intuitive, either. Our book explains how this game is played." The book is available at Amazon.com and itunes.apple.com for $9.95, and can also be purchased in print at www.amazon.com.

Van Herik Communications

Van Herik Communications provides strategic assessment and counsel on integrated communications for companies, nonprofit organizations and government agencies. It advises clients on how to develop PR campaigns to sway target audiences, including overall plan development, appropriate messaging and tactical implementation. Its award-winning staffers have helped clients in the real estate, finance, nonprofit and energy industries. For more information, please go to www.vanherikcommunications.com.

Fitzgerald PR Inc.

Fitzgerald PR is an award-winning PR firm dedicated to delivering value to business leaders who want to communicate positive news and information to the audiences that matter most in their industries. Founded by Debbie Graham Fitzgerald and husband Tim Fitzgerald in 2003, the firm employees reach both consumer and business-to-business audiences in numerous industries. Find more information at www.fitzgeraldpr.com.

###

FOR IMMEDIATE RELEASE

CONTACT:

Ed Van Herik
Van Herik Communications
404.431.1798
Ed@vanherikcommunications.com

PR PROS UNVEIL GREATEST MEDIA RELATIONS BOOK EVER WRITTEN

Book Tells What Companies Need to Know to Work with Journalists

ATLANTA, February XX, 2014 — Veteran public relations professionals Ed Van Herik and Debbie Graham Fitzgerald have outlined what organizations need to know if they want to expand their business and avoid missteps in dealing with reporters and editors.

Written in an engaging style, their 154-page book, *Megaphones Be With You,* details how a company can decide if it has news, how to work with reporters, how to get coverage for a company or nonprofit even if they don't have news, and how to assess return on investment.

"Many businesses and nonprofits would like to boost their image through positive coverage, but they either don't know where to begin or they've tried and failed," said Debbie Graham Fitzgerald, CEO of Fitzgerald PR in Atlanta. "We lead them through the process of determining if a media relations program will be worthwhile and give them the information they need to develop a successful media campaign."

The book, nicknamed "The Greatest Media Relations Book Ever Written," uses an analytical approach, enlivened by real-life examples, to demonstrate:

- How to assess an organization's potential for getting media coverage;
- How to pick the appropriate media outlets and reporters;
- How to approach journalists effectively;
- How to leverage social media to maximize coverage;
- How to determine ROI.

"*Megaphones Be With You* describes how journalists look at their jobs, how to plug in to their existing mindset, and how to assess the various media opportunities available today," said Ed Van Herik, founder of Van Herik Communications in Atlanta. "This isn't rocket science, but it isn't intuitive, either. Our book explains how this game is played." The book is available at Amazon.com and itunes.apple.com for $9.95, and can also be purchased in print at www.amazon.com.

Van Herik Communications

Van Herik Communications provides strategic assessment and counsel on integrated communications for companies, nonprofit organizations and government agencies. It advises clients on how to develop PR campaigns to sway target audiences, including overall plan development, appropriate messaging and tactical implementation. Its award-winning staffers have helped clients in the real estate, finance, nonprofit and energy industries. For more information, please go to www.vanherikcommunications.com.

Fitzgerald PR Inc.

Fitzgerald PR is an award-winning PR firm dedicated to delivering value to business leaders who want to communicate positive news and information to the audiences that matter most in their industries. Founded by Debbie Graham Fitzgerald and husband Tim Fitzgerald in 2003, the firm employees reach both consumer and business-to-business audiences in numerous industries. Find more information at www.fitzgeraldpr.com.

###

Our main advice to you, when reading a release written by an experienced PR professional, is to review for accuracy versus reading to rewrite. We know a review of a release can be rather subjective, so don't be one of those people to hold up the completion of a release because of a creative difference. Also, we write using The Associated Press Stylebook—a style and usage guide used by newspapers and in the news industry in the United States. Basically, if we don't write using these guidelines, the media will need to edit what we send them. And we don't want to turn them away from being receptive to our future work if they consider us unprofessional.

Have faith in the process and let the practitioner continue on to the next step: to distribute the release and garner some positive publicity.

The Media Alert

A media alert is basically an invitation to the media to attend and cover an upcoming event or press conference. It offers all the details: *who, what, where, when,* and *why.* Additionally, it will have a list of the spokespersons available for interview as well as give an idea of what kind of visual elements will be interesting to capture for a photo or video shoot. Consider the following example:

Media Alert

EXPERTS TO OUTLINE SECRETS
TO SUCCESS WITH THE MEDIA

Megaphones Be With You Authors Describe How It Is Done

WHAT	Authors of the book, *Megaphones Be With You, The Best Media Relations Book Ever Written,* will be outlining how to engage with the media successfully to benefit businesses and nonprofits at a free workshop next Thursday. The award-winning media professionals will outline key steps in media relations from deciding what's news, what to say to a reporter, and how to cut through today's communications clutter to reach key journalists.
WHEN	Thursday, Nov. 5, 2015, from 9:30 a.m. to 1 p.m.
WHERE	Downtown Civic Center, 1224 Main St., Anywhere, USA.
WHO	Authors Ed Van Herik of Van Herik Communications and Debbie Graham Fitzgerald of Fitzgerald PR.
VISUALS	Shots of presenters, visual props and of the audience.
CONTACT	Debbie Graham Fitzgerald Fitzgerald PR Debbie@fitzgeraldpr.com 770.887.6060 Ed Van Herik Van Herik Communications ed@vanherikcommunications.com 404.431.1798

Visuals

Visuals add another dimension to each story. For some media, like television, imagery is essential. While people once joked that every TV newscast showed at least one raging fire, they had a point: Audiences prefer watching descriptive video and photos over looking at a spokesperson attempt to describe the flames while he or she stands behind a podium. Therefore, enhance your media coverage by offering high-resolution photos and video opportunities. Media relations experts are regularly involved in the task of coordinating photo shoots with the help of a professional photographer. Likewise, they would advise you to keep standard shots readily available along with other images, including graphs, to demonstrate your pitch.

Similar principles apply to the web. Many organizations prepare and post short videos on YouTube to use with their releases. Additionally, to make that vital connection with their target audiences, successful web pages further make clever use of pertinent graphics to entice visitors to stay a few more seconds.

Web opportunities have also produced a hybrid release, often called a social media release, that incorporates photos, video, audio and type in a package made available to print, TV, web and radio reporters. A social media release is especially helpful to journalists, who can quickly and easily put each element to work when pushing to meet multiple deadlines in different media.

Ed Van Herik

Media relations is an imprecise science; sometimes the unexpected happens. Once, while representing a major overseas tire maker, I arranged for photos and video to be taken when the company announced a soccer sports sponsorship during a prominent game. Media in the United States weren't interested, but in the multinational's home country, every TV station wanted that tape. It turned out that the tire company was under fire for labor issues in an Asian country, and the tape was part of a "good story" that would offset the impact to the company's image in its home nation.

Distribution Strategy

Consider how you will distribute your release. Who are the target audiences? Which publications, TV shows and blogs do they follow? How will journalists receive the release?

Executives of certain organizations, most often nonprofits, know the key reporters and, consequently, what to expect from their associated news outlets. Even so, the media scene changes rapidly and reporters move frequently.

To keep track of the changes, PR practitioners use databanks with information on thousands of journalists and bloggers, covering every aspect of the news. In addition, a number of newswires, many of national scope, distribute news releases for free or a price. An online search for *press release distribution* will yield a list of potential vendors.

When using a distribution service, an organization should ask fundamental questions about target markets: Who are the target audiences? How do they receive their information? Which newswire shows the best promise of reaching them?

Numerous newswire options range from large distributors—certainly the veterans like PR Newswire and Business Wire—which provide a host of ancillary services to publicize a release to budget distributors and free online services.

Press Conferences

What if you gave a press conference and no one came? Even with the promise of a compelling topic, journalists can be pulled off the assignment to catch a breaking story. Predicting what the media will cover on any given day is impossible. An organization can submit media alerts to TV and newspapers weeks in advance, but unexpected events often trump press conferences at the last moment.

Helplessly standing by as your CEO prepares to talk to an empty room is every media professional's nightmare; that outcome is one you should dread as well. It may be possible to salvage coverage by calling media outlets afterward, telling them the CEO is still available for interviews, but it still will reflect poorly on the decision to hold the press event in the first place.

Ed Van Herik

In one situation, a PR professional was convinced her well-coordinated press conference would be a hit. No one could predict, though, that a city resident with personal problems would steal a 57-ton military tank and cut a path of destruction for nearly 30 minutes through a quiet San Diego neighborhood. Every TV crew in the city was sucked into the coverage, and the press conference was a bust.

Research: Finding Stories in Which to Appear

Essentially, pursuing one of two alternatives will help you appear in the news: one, to pitch the press when your organization originates a newsworthy story; two, to respond when opportunities arise to appear in media stories that showcase your organization in a good light.

Although responding sometimes means being ready when a journalist calls, it is also possible to be proactive by looking for stories to appear in. For example, by searching various online resources, you can potentially uncover a number of pertinent story opportunities. Even better, some media engagement opportunities come directly from media people.

- HARO (Help a Reporter Out™) uses an email distribution list to broadcast requests from reporters seeking sources for their stories. For example, if a reporter needs the expertise of an engineer who builds bridges, he or she will post a notice on HARO, which is sent to thousands of recipients nationwide. Likewise, at the time of this writing, according to HARO's website, nearly 30,000 members of the media have cited HARO sources in their work. For that reason, PR professionals also scan HARO in search of opportunities for their clients, but anybody on the planet has access.

Ed Van Herik

Even if your company is in a very specialized niche, finding media opportunities on HARO can be possible. Recently, I asked for sources for a freelance story I was writing on churches that set up only on weekends. I received seven pertinent responses and included three in the final article.

- ProfNet, a paid service owned by PR Newswire, is used daily by hundreds of reporters seeking sources for their stories. ProfNet allows only qualified PR professionals to view reporter queries, so the pitches are more skilled. Although HARO has grown more widely popular, ProfNet is also quite viable.

Debbie Graham Fitzgerald

Having pitched both HARO and ProfNet, and garnered many hits, I love this forum of using technology to allow the journalist to reach out and ask for help! A few years ago, a physical fitness trainer's story was turned into feature articles for several national women's magazines simply by pitching queries from HARO and ProfNet. The magazines had money to produce lavish photo shoots (with assistants, hair/makeup professionals and fashion stylists) at the trainer's studio, and the results yielded more than 37 million impressions for my client.

At this point, you might feel that landing a feature story requires nearly as much effort as you exerted to accomplish the newsworthy feat in the first place. Such sentiments are understandable. Your time and other resource commitments, however, should pay off.

To win the season, a strong football team doesn't necessarily need a cheerleading captain and squad. Besides, those pompoms aren't free—they come with their own operating rules and resource requirements! Nevertheless, the players are more likely to score points if supported by cheerleaders who, working together like pros, inspire fans to fill the stadium and root for the team. And that's especially true if the other teams have great cheerleaders.

Key Points:

- The press release follows a standard, reporter-friendly format that remains popular with newsmakers and media personnel.

- The media alert is an invitation to the media to cover an event.

- High-resolution images, including video, add an important dimension to news stories, so organizations should keep digitized supporting photos and other visuals on file for quick access.

- Access to media database services ensures that media information, including appropriate contact information, is current.

- Executives often like press conferences, but they have their own perils.

- Online services like HARO efficiently pair experts who desire press with reporters who need legitimate sources.

CHAPTER 8

Show Time: The Media Interview

When a media representative calls for an interview—or an *on-the-record* conversation in industry terms—it's show time.

The opportunity usually arises when a journalist is under deadline pressure. An industry development prompts a need for an expert's reaction, so the journalist calls an organization's spokesperson for a comment. At that moment, the reporter wants an instant assessment in clear, unqualified sentences.

If your spokesperson needs some time to think about what to say, the individual should first ask about the deadline and then request the remaining questions.

Taking a timeout is OK. Assuming you are the contact, offer to call back in five minutes if the deadline is immediate. Write down your thoughts and reply within the promised time frame. You might be asked to make a prediction—perhaps about the impact of a new development in your industry. If you're unsure, then say so, or use words like *might, could* or *possibly.*

The PR value of being positioned as the expert before hundreds of potential customers can be enormous, although the advantages come with certain inconveniences and frustrations. A call to respond could arrive at the start of a child's first soccer game or during a high-priority meeting. Nevertheless, most trusted sources realize that the impressions they create by being known as the authority benefit their organizations in many ways. They make the personal sacrifices so that, optimally, readers and viewers associate the organization with a name they can trust and turn to that source for business.

Speak up.

While the reporter is seemingly in charge of the interview, your spokesperson should not be bashful about inserting the organization's key talking points into the conversation. Reporters want expertise, so tell them what's important and why.

A company, for instance, unveils a new software product. The spokesperson, therefore, says: "Our latest development will transform the way our customers

Debbie Graham Fitzgerald

Journalists are under tight deadlines daily, but as a media relations expert my goal is to divert those queries. I want to field the calls first in order to qualify the media, get as much information as I can about the story, and ask for particular questions the reporters are looking to get answered. That way, I can track down and prepare my client (e.g., discuss story topic, develop talking points) for an interview within the timeframe given. Additionally, I coordinate the media interview (via conference call, or in person) and listen in—doing what I call being my client's conscience—in order to make sure all talking points are covered and to also chime in if any red flag comments are made by my client. (Compliance issues and proprietary information that need to be protected could come into play.) Obviously, I have already media trained my client; however, during these interviews I take extensive notes (I type fast!) and always follow up with feedback. Being the middleman like this for my clients has worked well for thousands of interviews over my career.

store data. We expect our mid-size customers to save as much as 30 percent a year." The statement builds up the company, but since the savings could be important to audiences, a journalist covering the topic might report the figure.

If you make similar statements, expect any good journalist to question your assertions. Be prepared, then, to back up your projections with facts without revealing confidential data. Don't give away more than necessary. Emphasize what's important and, when asked, deliver supporting material.

Realize that the reporter isn't likely to use a message point that simply promotes the company unless the opinion relates to the entire story. As a rule, your spokesperson's points are not sales pitches; they demonstrate expertise in the field.

Keep the points in plain view.

Put your three message points—or talking points— in writing. Assuming you are the spokesperson, have the prompts in plain view (on a screen or on paper) during the phone interview. Although a media interview often wanders like a conversation, the exchange of information is a transaction. For that reason, approach each media interaction with the same care as any other business opportunity. Don't make it up as you go along.

At the same time, strive to be engaging during the interview. Also understanding that the reporter is looking for information, not a hard time, it helps to

Debbie Graham Fitzgerald

When preparing for a client to talk to media, I like to understand the reason behind the news they are discussing and the authenticity in the story. For instance, I provided media relations for a fledgling San Francisco tech company during the dot-com boom. The company created a safe and secure online website just for kids. Interestingly, the CEO of the company, a grandmother of eight, developed the new type of website. Her company was also backed by a large technology firm with tens of millions of dollars, so needless to say, the top tier tech and entertainment media (including People magazine) responded to my "High-Tech Grandma" pitches and wanted interviews. Did the stories simply just talk about the product itself and how it was a 100 percent safe site for kids to play on the Internet? No! Media curiosity, as I expected, was on how a grandmother incubated the idea because she desired a safe online experience for her grandchildren.

keep an open mind if a journalist asks questions that seem off the topic. Gathering information—more than what will end up in the story—is part of the journalist's job. If the conversation strays too far, the spokesperson should gently steer the interviewer back to main talking points.

Finally, have realistic expectations. Getting only one message point into a news story is a terrific outcome. With some planning, the organization's primary point becomes the one in print.

Debbie Graham Fitzgerald

Consider what happens behind the scenes when a reporter under a tight deadline reaches out to me: First, I track down my client spokesman No. 1 (at the office, airport, on the golf course, driving in the car, or eating somewhere). If client spokesman No. 1 can do the interview, I begin the prepping. If spokesman No. 1 can't do the job, then I track down spokesman No. 2. Time is of the essence. Consequently, I groom my clients always to be prepared for a last-minute media opportunity call from their media relations professional.

Key Points:

- Journalists tend to approach their trusted sources for on-the-record comments when deadlines are imminent.

- Serving as the media's go-to source for expertise can pose challenges, but committed spokespeople see the value in building favor among target audiences, who will one day make decisions about supporting the nonprofit or business.

- Spokespeople should be well-prepared to emphasize important points and, when asked, provide supporting material.

- While key points can place the organization in a positive light, they should not come across as a self-serving sales pitch.

CHAPTER 9

A View From the Other Side

How do journalists decide whether to cover a story?

First thing in the morning and later in the afternoon, top editors gather to discuss what they'll cover that day. Stories include a combination of hard news—politicians getting arrested, big fires, or what we've heard a popular magazine editor say, "death, divorce and destruction"— and soft news—features, staged media events, neighborhood happenings. Typically, journalists look for a mix to ensure they report the major news of the day as well as present topics for nearly every sensibility.

If you're curious about the process, look behind the scenes. Stations like WXIA-TV in Atlanta stream their news conferences live every day. The public can listen in on editors as they discuss the news of the day and the way the elements fit together; people can also comment on the editors' choices by email in real time.

As a matter of fact, the editorial discussions reveal just why no one knows how much media a press conference will draw until the day of the event: We can't predict what will happen from one moment to the next.

Consequently, if the decision is made to unveil news at an event, most media relations professionals recommend hosting a stand-alone event—one designed to attract community leaders, elected officials, and even people off the street. The media, of course, receive invitations, but if journalists do not show up, the occasion should be well-attended by others.

Key Points:

- Daily news organizations strive to cover a mix of stories—from the most relevant hot news to a number of special topics—to satisfy their broad audiences.

- Breaking news can demand scheduling changes throughout any day.

- To ensure their events are well-attended, even if breaking news waylays reporters, PR professionals recommend planning press conferences that draw public figures and others in addition to journalists. Then, take good photos and/or video to leverage with the media after the event.

CHAPTER 10

Other PR: Tactics That Complement Media Relations

We often think that succeeding in public relations and getting media coverage are synonymous, but organizations use a number of other tactics to become better known. The other PR activities, in fact, can present reasons to reach out to the media.

Speaking Engagements

A speaking engagement can provide a prime opportunity to expose your organization's expertise to a targeted audience, build your brand image, and generate client, customer or supporter leads through networking. Whether your executive speaks to a small group of business professionals or to thousands of attendees at a prominent industry conference, you'll make the most of the engagement through preparation and promotion.

Speaking engagements generally fall under one of two categories: 1) the traditional engagement that involves a pitch to get booked at an event, and 2) the engagement an organization plans and prepares on its own. In either situation, the basics of how to promote the speaking engagement via media relations are the same.

Traditional speaking engagements are obtained by pitching someone, such as the organizer's event planner. The goal of the pitch is to secure a spot for an executive to present. The event itself could be a trade show, business association meeting, and/or other venue. Typically, the following positions exist:

- Sole speaker - One speaker delivers a message, and the presentation serves as the main event. The individual could be a keynote speaker or a topic presenter.

- Panelist participant - Several professionals take part in a panel discussion, often with a moderator who fields questions from the audience. The format tends to be less formal and generally requires less preparation than a solo speaking engagement.

The following tips are useful if you aim to land a traditional gig:

- Build a list of important events that reach your target audience. Choose the top five or 10 on which you want to focus.

- Contact event planners six to 12 months prior to an event. Planning takes place far in advance, and competition for speaking slots can be intense.

- Have a hot topic. The most relevant relate to current events or trends. Provide meaningful information, insight or tips—and a fresh perspective—to avoid repeating what other experts have offered to the marketplace.

- Look for free speaking opportunities. Some conferences require a paid sponsorship to get on the speaker agenda, but many do not. Costs to speak primarily depend on the industry. In some instances, speakers can obtain certain benefits, such as a free conference passes and travel fees, so be sure to inquire about perks.

Debbie Graham Fitzgerald

After pitching the planners of an international private equity conference held in Europe, they were deeply interested in my client being a speaker. After inquiring about waiving the conference fees, they agreed and also offered two free conference passes to solidify the engagement. It's a good thing I asked— my client saved more than $4,000 on conference fees.

Some organizations plan and budget their own engagements, generally falling under the categories of workshops and seminars. Durations vary according to each event's purpose, which would include targeting a key audience and, therefore, designing the ambiance of the event to appeal directly to that group.

Online speaking engagements are also gaining popularity. Although they aren't gathered in the same physical venue, audience members can interact with the speaker via phone, Internet chats and online posts.

You could pitch to speak for another organization's online event or host your own:

- Webinars - Short for *web-based seminars*, webinars are not only heavily promoted within industry publications and trade association communications, but they are widely popular vehicles for sharing information.

- Vlogs – Short for *video blogs*, they combine the online journal—the blog—with the medium of video to create a form of web television. Vlogs can be uploaded to video-sharing websites, such as YouTube, or web syndication services, like RSS (Rich Site Summary), to broaden their reach to audiences.

- Podcasts – A name derived from the portability of the iPod, the web-based broadcasts, whether audio or visual, are often syndicated via RSS feeds or other distribution websites. Likewise, podcasts are widely available as downloads on smart phones and TVs.

- YouTube channels and other online networks.

Debbie Graham Fitzgerald

My smart TV gives me immediate access to the Internet, including YouTube channels, via my high-definition big screen television. I'll browse whatever topic interests me (many are educational) to watch videos—all with the click of a remote!

One item to note here: Webinars, vlogs and podcasts are considered a form of content creation, a role specialized PR professionals are highly capable of developing for their clients.

Whether to help your organization's executives land traditional speaking engagements or host events, an experienced media relations professional can often leverage the most benefit from either type of public relations by providing the following kinds of support:

- Ghostwriting the speech and helping with visual elements.

- Promoting and building attendance for the event.

- Inviting media to attend and cover the event.

- Capturing great photos (still shots or video).

- Writing a post-event press release and distributing the piece with a photo and/or video.

In short, the right speaking engagements can open up new worlds of business for any company and solidify its position of expertise. An investment of time and other resources can provide a significant return.

Bylined Articles

Have you ever read an article written by someone you know and thought, *hey, how'd he get to write for that publication?* Media relations professionals commonly get that question. Luckily, how to publish articles is not a big mystery. Success, nevertheless, follows a step-by-step process.

Known in the media world as a bylined article, the informative piece is written for a key audience and a specific publication. *Byline* distinguishes that the article includes the author's name. Numerous opportunities exist to author pieces for reputable publications. Publishers regularly seek guest columnists to help satisfy their constant need for good editorial content, including contributed articles and opinion pieces.

When granted a bylined article, the executive gains the opportunity to showcase the organization's knowledge and drive key messages to key target audiences. The primary benefit—establishing credibility as an expert—builds trust and identifies the organization as the experienced adviser. Appearing in outside publications usually helps the visibility of the organization's website as well.

Delivering a successful bylined article follows certain dos and don'ts:

DOs

- Determine an appropriate topic and the right expert for the bylined article.

- Before writing the article, pitch the idea to the publication's editor in charge of reviewing and accepting guest articles. Two good reasons: First, you won't waste time on a piece that has no chance of running. Second, an editor appreciates having input at the beginning.

- Once your organization receives the editor's go-ahead, research all of the publication's required specifications so that you write the article in the publication's style. At the same time, adhere to the other stipulations: word count, preferred format, and deadline.

- Write the article to inform, not to sell the audience. Editors want opinions, how-to's, trends, and forward-thinking content that interest and enlighten readers.

- If the appointed executive does not like to write or have the time, let a media relations professional interview the individual and ghostwrite the first draft. Making edits from a preliminary manuscript is far easier than beginning with a blank page.

Editors approve of bylined articles that are ghostwritten, and the commonplace practice among busy executives saves time. However, the content should originate from the organization and the executive.

Article Guidelines:

- Give credit where credit is due by making footnotes or citing sources in your article.

- Submit a high-resolution professional photo with the article.

- Prepare to take advantage of the publicity by staying in touch with the editor regarding article's slated publication date. The operative word here is *slated*; the media offer no guarantees, especially if breaking news bumps the story.

- Determine if the executive owns the article. Most publications retain the copyright to their published articles. In that case, the organization can often purchase reprints to leverage the work via other marketing and public relations tactics. In certain situations, editors give permission to reuse the article. For example, the organization might be allowed to distribute the piece to an internal database of contacts without purchasing a reprint as long as the original publication receives proper credit.

Debbie Graham Fitzgerald

When I met with the CPA owner of an accounting firm, he admitted that the idea of writing conjured thoughts of scratching fingernails down a chalkboard. You should have seen him squirm just thinking about the prospect of drafting an article. Hearing his confession, I revealed I hated bookkeeping and preparing taxes as much as he hated writing. We both hired each other's firms to eliminate those tasks that caused us so much pain.

DON'Ts

- Don't expect payment for a contributed article.

- When pitching, if your organization is advertising in the publication, don't mention that point to the editor. Doing so is a real turnoff. Reputable editors do not care who advertises. If the content is right for a publication, editors with high standards and ethics consider articles for their merit alone.

- Don't use industry jargon. If including certain terminology is important, the executive should briefly explain such references in context.

- Don't be boring.

Once you and other executives from your organization join the ranks of authors who have bylined articles, you'll realize that what you needed to do was no mystery after all. A certain mystique, however, will likely follow *you*. In fact, get ready to be approached by clients and industry colleagues: *Hey, I saw your article. How did you get to write for that publication?*

Awards and Lists

Gaining recognition in your industry by earning awards and appearing on top/best lists deliver legitimate reasons to promote those accolades to your target audiences.

Awards

All types of awards are given to organizations and individuals as a way of recognizing their excellence in

Debbie Graham Fitzgerald

"We won! And beat out the competition!" Those were the golden words written in an email from a managing director of a mergers and acquisitions firm. He sent the good news to the entire firm minutes after he accepted an industry award. Those words were also my green light to send out the press release I had already prepared for the client.

their professions and industries. Professional associations and media publications are among many organizations that produce award celebrations to commemorate excellence.

Lists

Most city's business journals and magazines recognize leaders in select industries throughout the year. Editorial calendars are filled with them. Daily newspapers and online publications also employ similar lists:

- Top 25 Firms in (Your industry)
- Top 40 under 40
- Best Places to Work

Requirements to submit entries, including completing all of the forms with documentation, can be time-consuming, so plan ahead to meet the deadlines. You might also encounter fees associated with submitting your entry, but the costs are usually minimal and reasonable.

Something to consider: Organizations that originate such awards and lists are keenly motivated to sell seats to their events and ad space in their publications. You should not be obligated to attend the awards celebration or purchase advertisements to win. However, showing up could be a smart move. Many such events provide great networking opportunities with industry peers. Contacts made by being present could elevate your organization's profile and boost your bottom line.

Key Points:

- Speaking engagements expose an organization's expertise to a targeted audience, build the brand's image, and generate client, customer or patron leads through networking.

- In addition to speaking in person, online opportunities—webinars, vlogs, podcasts, YouTube—deliver exposure to highly targeted groups.

- Bylined articles in respected publications position executives as industry experts and, in turn, enhance the credibility of their organizations.

- Gaining recognition from earning awards or landing on best-of lists delivers a wide range of PR opportunities along with direct exposure to contacts that become significant to an organization.

CHAPTER 11

When a Crisis Hits

Any reputable business or nonprofit executive dreads the day when something terribly bad happens: A faulty product injures a customer. The company's most visible representative makes a gaffe. A fire erupts at the local plant.

Suddenly, dozens of pressing matters erupt, and, yes, talking to media should be among the leadership's top concerns. Unquestionably, executives are the ones responsible for acknowledging in public what occurred and explaining what the company is doing about the problem. Even so, many are tempted to brush off the media.

Why is that?

The urgency of other priorities can make the job of managing the press feel like a nuisance rather than a necessity. While that's the explanation many give and, on some level, believe to be true, the deeper reason some executives avoid the media during times of crisis stems from their insecurities. Those who aren't comfortable with the media rationalize the importance of sticking to operational issues that fall within familiar territory, and they feel justified in focusing on their areas of expertise.

No matter what a crisis entails, however, the media provide the quickest, most effective means for an organization to inform customers, suppliers, supporters, and the general public about what is going on and how everyone is affected. As a matter of fact, by communicating through the media, the nonprofit or enterprise potentially gains a powerful opportunity to demonstrate its capabilities and efficiencies. Also, stakeholders, wanting answers, end up judging the organization in crisis by the quality of the leadership's responses.

Further, the media won't go away simply because a beleaguered CEO or executive team declines to talk to them. With no other option, journalists go to competitors, neighbors and public officials for quotes about the organization's plight.

Few would argue that taking charge of your own story is always best. Stepping up, however, means being willing to talk right away, generally before your key personnel have a firm grasp on the extent of the crisis. Concerns over speaking inappropriately, therefore, are understandable and warranted.

By following some guidelines, you can satisfy the press and avoid misspeaking before you have complete answers:

- Begin by telling them what you know, however little that might be, and then tell them what you're doing to find out more. Give them a short description of what the crisis is, and how it will affect current customers and the general public.

- Avoid speculation. Don't create more of a crisis by giving the media a reason to believe the event could be more dramatic than current facts indicate.

- Don't minimize. People have a tendency to hide pertinent bad news during a crisis simply because the situation sounds awful. While the tendency to conceal the ugly truth is a natural reaction, any kind of deceit will come back to haunt the company. The facts always emerge in time, and the media can be merciless if they think they were misled. And hiding bad news, even for a day or two, will cause the story to drag on, hurting the company even more.

The previous guidelines will come in handy, but they are starting points. Imagine trying to think of suitable answers on the spot while journalists fire off questions during a crisis. To prepare ahead, most media relations professionals advise companies to prepare a crisis communications plan. Often part of a larger disaster recovery plan, the crisis communications component outlines how outreach will be handled during a crisis.

Generally, a crisis communication plan outlines: a) typical disaster scenarios along with talking points, b) a process to notify key company and community officials, and c) a protocol to get information from key officers to the company spokesperson and to the media and community.

Most companies avoid drafting a business recovery plan, much less a plan to talk to the media, when everything is going south. Still, developing such a strategy is among the unpleasant tasks your organization

Debbie Graham Fitzgerald

Be prepared when a crisis hits and especially be aware of investigative reporters. You know the ones that will chase people through hallways, parking lots, etc., trying to get a comment. Don't be that person being chased. I always cringe when I see that on the news. Instead, be prepared—even if only a two-sentence, preplanned statement. Write it, memorize it and then give that reporter the contact number to your crisis PR professional.

should suck up and do. If ever needed, the plan could save you and your entire operation.

Important note: While placing the boss in the position of media spokesperson is tempting, he or she might not be the best choice. The CEO might better

Ed Van Herik

At Super Bowl 2003 in San Diego, the local utility was concerned about the electrical system at the stadium. To prepare, they stationed crews there and asked me to handle media in case the lights went out. They estimated that it would take five minutes to determine the problem if an outage should occur. Before the game, I told stadium personnel in the press box that I would hold a briefing within five minutes in the press tent in the parking lot if the lights went out. I then prepared five minutes' worth of briefing materials, giving me 10 minutes to get a briefing from the crews. We were prepared but nothing happened, though I did get to see Tampa Bay whomp the Raiders 48-21. No communications plan, however, was in place when the lights went out at Super Bowl 2013, leaving football announcers fumbling for something to say while the nation—and the teams—waited for repairs.

be utilized by coordinating restoration efforts, even if the media wants to talk to him or her. In some cases, they can make brief appearances during the crisis while leaving the day-to-day or hour-to-hour briefings to a media-savvy staffer.

Clearly, no one wants to imagine all of the potential calamities that could hit at any point in the future. However, just as various insurance policies mitigate tangible and intangible losses resulting from unforeseen events, crisis communication plans keep damages under control and help restore an organization's overall position. A company that exudes confidence and competence throughout a crisis has the best chance of recovering and building goodwill.

Key Points:

- Among all of the priorities an organization faces when a crisis hits, communicating with the media remains near the top of the list.

- Although many executives downplay their role in reaching out to the media during a crisis and even attempt to avoid public comments, they quickly realize that journalists seeking answers will get them one way or another.

- Taking charge of your organization's story requires providing thoughtful responses throughout a crisis.

- A crisis communications plan functions like an insurance policy—mitigating damage and restoring an organization to a position of strength.

- While an executive is often the first one chosen to stand before the media as the organization's spokesperson, such individuals, who typically have more pressing business, should sometimes turn the job over to communications personnel.

CHAPTER 12

Having a Media Relations Pro on Your Side: More Valuable Than You Think

PR and Journalism Ethics

No law requires journalists or public relations practitioners to be honest or accurate, but ethical codes guide both professions. Even so, reporters and PR pros, at times, make mistakes and interpret events or information from viewpoints that differ from newsmakers. And, in certain cases, misrepresentations are willful.

Still, professional principles call for reporters to be fair to both sides in disputes and for PR professionals to be accurate when promoting their clients. In short, ethical codes call for both to be honest with the public, and true professionals take those standards seriously.

The Public Relations Society of America (PRSA), maintaining a code of ethics for members, proclaims: "We adhere to the highest standards of accuracy and truth in advancing the interests of those we represent and in communicating with the public."

In fact, PRSA helps practitioners learn how to be ethical and to detect, deter and avoid unethical behavior. Fake product reviews, nondisclosure of interests represented, plagiarism, unpaid internships, and standards for aggregation and ethics in blogging are just a few of the topics PRSA discusses with its members.

For several reasons, reputable PR practitioners are obliged to tell the media the truth about a nonprofit's or business's issues, even when the news is not flattering. First, lying isn't a business strategy; conveying anything but the truth is dishonest. Second, beyond the simple ethical issue lies the practical reality: It is hard to lie consistently and not get caught, especially in the face of intense media scrutiny.

BP's 2010 Deepwater Horizon oil spill in the Gulf of Mexico presents a classic case of a company attempting to minimize a disaster that would become the biggest accidental marine oil spill to date. Commonly referred to as the "BP disaster" or "BP oil spill," the explosion killed 11 people working on the rig, releasing a sea-floor gusher that spewed oil for 87 days. After the fact, federal criminal charges were filed against BP, which pled guilty to multiple offenses, including lying to Congress. In light of the facts, the executive decision to play down the catastrophe now seems incredible.

While reputable PR practitioners always put the best face on organizational news, they are scrupulous in their efforts to avoid giving out false information or creating a misleading impression. They know from experience that today's emphasis on transparency means that lies are often uncovered, and the harm resulting from deceiving the public about bad news can be far worse than the pain of the injury alone.

Upon revealing lies, the media no longer believe a company's statements—at least not for a long, long time—and reporters are not the only parties affected. Arguably, the media can't control people's thoughts and decisions, but journalists can sway current or prospective customers and supporters. All in all, a string of negative articles about a company or nonprofit is more likely to hurt than help an organization.

As a practical matter, PR professionals can draw from dozens of ways to present information. Sifting through all

Debbie Graham Fitzgerald

If a client ever asked me to spin the truth in a way that would deceive the public, I would do whatever I could to dissuade the principals from their line of thinking. If they still insisted on being deceptive, I'd have no other choice but to resign from the account.

Ed Van Herik

I once took a call from a reporter asking about an asbestos cleanup project underway at a client's facility. I went to a company technical adviser for an answer and relayed his reassuring information to the reporter, on air. Later, the reporter found out the site had been shut down by government officials. I didn't know a thing about the shutdown, but my interview gave the impression that I had tried to mislead the reporter. As a result, I told the client I would no longer represent them to the media on the issue, which ended up in federal court.

of their options, experts in the business of media relations formulate the best possible ways to reveal bad news.

Key Points:

- Professional associations guide media professionals, but miscommunications and mistakes can still happen.

- Organizations are more likely to contain the impact of a negative event when executives and media relations specialists address the bad news publically as early as possible.

CHAPTER 13

When You May be the Victim of Unfair Reporting

By far, the majority of journalists are dedicated, objective professionals, just trying their best to report the truth of the day. But not all are like that. Some practice "gotcha" journalism, whereby a good story means that someone gets nailed. Oftentimes as well, overwhelmed journalists simply get their interpretations or facts wrong, injuring an innocent story subject.

How, then, does an organization deal effectively with internal perceptions that a story was not fair?

If you're in this position, start by getting a reality check on the story. Many executives perceive any story that reflects poorly on their efforts to be in error. But, to be fair, some harsh stories are valid. Therefore, first make sure that the seemingly unfair story really is. Ask friends, neighbors, and others trusted in the industry for their opinions. Confirm that you have a legitimate case before attempting to argue before an unsympathetic audience. In short, don't drink the Kool-Aid that lulls you into believing your organization is perfect.

Instead, determine if the story contains information that is verifiably wrong or if the interpretation of the facts is askew. If the reporter didn't get the facts right, then the conversation with that person should be a short one. Any reputable news organization will publish a correction. However, if the information in the article is correct but the company doesn't agree with the reporter's interpretation, then the process of influencing any action becomes significantly more difficult.

Reporters readily defend their interpretations, especially if derived from quotes and materials they've obtained from other industry spokespeople. As far as journalists in such positions are concerned, those kinds of discrepancies boil down to competing views, both of which they will contend were presented. While a company can maintain that the other side's argument is wrong, that point won't cause a publication to print a correction. Raising the issue, however, might prompt reporters and publishers to seek a different view the next time they do an article.

Further, to be effective in challenging a journalist or media outlet with a bias complaint, executives of enterprises and nonprofits need to take the journalist's mindset into account when presenting their claims. *The tone of the broadcast wasn't fair,* for instance, has no substance and, therefore, will not sway a journalist who frequently hears similarly broad complaints.

What, then, will cause journalists to take a bias complaint seriously? Facts will. Remember that mainstream journalists are expected to produce stories that are fair and balanced. If they fail to cover all of the pertinent facts, then they are open to criticism, even by their own journalistic standards.

Beyond presenting evidence of missing or incorrect information, pinning down actual media bias in news articles can be quite complicated. One common complaint is over the amount of space allotted. While measuring a story in inches might seem a legitimate way to prove a contention of bias, offering an assessment of the story's comments is more relevant.

The following issues are among those that would cause a journalist to take your media bias complaint to heart:

You aren't called in time to prepare an adequate response for the story. In "gotcha" journalism, a common technique among journalists is to spend most of the newsgathering time writing the story as a hit piece and then waiting until the last hour before the story must be submitted to ask the target for detailed answers to several complex questions. Intended to make the process look fair, the ambush tactic generally serves a particular agenda.

If a one-sided story results under such a circumstance, then an organization has a shot at redress.

Your comments are shortened to the point of creating the wrong impression. If you were interviewed over the phone, proving that a reporter left out important elements of what you said can be difficult. If you communicated by email or a second person listened in on the interview, then the journalist will more likely take your complaint seriously. Many journalists, even those with utmost integrity, however, sometimes hear an argument about unfairness and believe the effort is an executive's attempt to cover a gaffe.

Your comments were taken out of context. While the contention could be true, proving that a journalist cherry-picked the words he or she used to make a point can be tough, even if the spokesperson can deliver proof of the full remark.

Your comments confirm facts about the story, but the other side's input condemns your actions. The situation creates a tricky predicament. The journalist can contend that you have received equal time when, in reality, you are not allotted the space to address the main issues of the article.

Generally, executives can expect newsrooms to view them as nonobjective; therefore, company spokespeople need to build an extremely firm case in order to prevail in a bias dispute.

A few words of caution: To begin, it always makes sense to review a reporter's work before granting an

Debbie Graham Fitzgerald

A client of mine had experienced a reporter taking his comments out of context during the height of the financial crisis. At the time, an article incited death threats from angry individuals towards the spokesperson, and the individual was further accused of contributing to the cause of the crisis. Unfortunately, when this spokesperson corresponded with that particular reporter, the interaction was: 1) against his instincts to talk to the reporter in the first place, but he only did so because his boss said to; and 2) he only had a one-on-one phone call with the reporter, so no one could verify what was said. In order to strategize moving forward, I needed to know this backstory, as it happened a year before he joined my client's firm. In future exchanges, I would always be on the phone with this spokesperson when he spoke with reporters. At the minimum, we would have proof of the conversation, as I take copious notes!

interview. The journalist's material can easily be found online, and determining up front whether you can expect to be represented fairly in the final news product

Ed Van Herik

I once attended a PTA party for my son's school, where an acquaintance approached me to say he knew who the local newspaper, my employer, secretly favored to win the next presidential election—based upon the photos the paper picked to run of each candidate. Supposedly, the chosen candidate had only the most flattering photos in the paper. As the night photo editor, I explained exactly how I picked those very photos, five nights a week. Each day we would run one picture of a candidate with the day's coverage of the campaign. After a couple of weeks, I was getting bored of seeing men in suits step off planes, so, to break up the monotony, I would choose a photo of, say, one of them reaching out to shake the hand of a well-wisher. The next day, I might use a photo of another in a polo shirt catching a ball. My selections had nothing to do with a conspiracy. No one had directed me to twist the coverage subtly through the photos. I was simply trying to add my contribution to an interesting overall news product.

is certainly worthwhile. Media relations professionals do exactly that before they make their recommendations to their clients.

124

Also, don't automatically assume a reporter is biased because you think their news organization has a political agenda. That means nothing to most reporters, who are simply trying to report the story accurately and quickly. Not always, but mostly.

Key Points:

- Organizations should be prepared to address media concerns when reporters play "gotcha" journalism and also when well-intentioned journalists make mistakes or omit points that lead to biased stories.

- Before issuing any complaint over a story, heads of organizations, who have their own biases, should take a realistic step back in evaluating whether or not a journalist should be confronted about a report and, if so, how.

- The easiest way to obtain a retraction is by proving that a reported statement is wrong.

- Aside from not receiving as much space or time as someone with an opposing view, an executive/company spokesperson seeking a retraction or the opportunity to offer an explanation must provide compelling reasons for a reporter to run a correction.

CHAPTER 14

Voicing Your Complaint to the News Outlet

To achieve solid results, an organization should take a systematic approach by which to address media bias. Answering questions that clarify what you aim to achieve by contacting the media is the first step:

- What does success look like?

- Is a correction good enough?

- Will the company settle for a clarification?

- Does the organization simply want to rattle the reporter for doing a lousy job?

Determining what constitutes a successful outcome takes some understanding of the media. The initial story, for instance, might have run with a bold headline and a big picture, but the correction probably won't receive the same prominent display. Most publications routinely place all amended statements in the same obscure area. Many who have rallied for retractions, therefore, are not only disappointed but feel like they've wasted their time upon finding the small correction buried at the bottom of page three next to an ad. Unfortunately, that's usually the reality.

If the reporter in question covers a company frequently, a fussy executive or media relations expert can sometimes rattle that person's cage just enough to prompt him or her to be more careful in the future. Journalists are in the business of reporting accurate news.

Ed Van Herik

As a reporter, I once covered a local businessman who enjoyed sparring with his partners in public—and didn't mind bouncing reporters up and down, too. The feisty guy had spooked another reporter so badly that the journalist started shying away from covering the businessman's activities.

They must justify their work to editors, so any assertion that reported information is false places journalists in the predicament of verifying all information more scrupulously. By their persistence, cranky executives have been known to intimidate reporters into handling their stories favorably.

Once you determine the ideal outcome, plan to speak directly with the person who wrote the story. Editors typically transfer calls about complaints to the responsible reporter.

Prepare for all kinds of reactions. Reporters tend to be defensive when confronted and frequently stonewall individuals who call to complain about stories. The less likely scenario is a journalist who, receptive to feedback, pleasantly surprises company and nonprofit spokespeople by a willingness to listen to objections. Since you can't predict someone's attitude in advance, outline your objections so that you speak calmly and evenly. The reporter's response will determine what steps to take next.

Scrupulous reporters and editors of reputable news organizations cherish their reputations for accuracy, so a quick response to clear up misinformation is standard policy. If your initial call to the reporter doesn't resolve the issue, ask to speak to an editor. An editor can overrule a reporter, and he or she should issue a correction if you demonstrate that your complaint has merit.

Ed Van Herik

Executives of one San Diego company were convinced that a local newspaper reporter who covered them was biased. Nevertheless, when factual errors made it into his stories, their quick call brought a quick correction. And it wasn't done grudgingly. If he had wrong information, the journalist made it a priority—right then—to alert his editor that a correction was coming.

All the same, you can't count on the second call—the one to the editor—going any more smoothly than the first. Editors, like reporters, hear from aggrieved story subjects routinely. While they won't necessarily brush off an executive, editors' reactions can be taken as snubs. If the desired outcome does not result, be prepared for an uphill struggle while contemplating and pursuing additional measures.

For one, the CEO or other important stakeholder could write a letter to the editor that outlines the perceived slant. While the editors are not obliged to print every letter, they often will run complaint letters to demonstrate their own openness. Keep in mind that the editorial submission should offer views and facts without running too long.

In addition to presenting the organization's side to the public, the communication also tells the publication's entire readership that at least one industry expert believes that particular reporter fails to do quality work. The reporter doesn't want that, and neither do his or her bosses.

All things considered, before submitting the letter, thoughtfully determine if dragging out the accusation

Ed Van Herik

I once had a client that was slammed in a Sunday editorial. I didn't know it was coming, and neither did the client. After contacting the newspaper, we:

1. *Demanded a correction for two minor factual errors, which we received.*
2. *Wrote a letter to the editor contesting the editorial, which ran the following Wednesday.*
3. *Pitched the op-ed page editor on running an op-ed (the articles that run on the page next to the editorials) representing my client's interpretation. I pointed out that the issue was topical because they were already writing about the subject. The op-ed article ran within 10 days of the original editorial.*

is in the organization's best interests. The shelf life of most news stories is hours, not days. The majority of audiences forget they heard or read the story by the next day. Today's newspaper *is* tomorrow's birdcage liner.

When evaluating the damage done, some will determine that the harm inflicted warrants fighting back with a lawsuit. In certain cases, such as when outrageous mistakes lead to major losses, going to court can be worth the effort. A word of caution: Don't expect editors to cave because your lawyer sent a letter. With experience in fighting suits and other legal allegations, large media organizations stand ready to defend their words and actions.

Key Points:

- Addressing media bias effectively requires a fact-based assessment of the situation and a coolheaded, goal-oriented strategy.

- Lodging a complaint starts with the reporter responsible for the story and only if no resolution results move up the ladder to the editor in charge.

- If the media outlet refuses to publish corrections or run a follow-up story, submitting an opinion letter to the editor from the organization's CEO can be an effective way of presenting points to the publication's audience.

- Whether voicing complaints, submitting letters to the editors for publication, or taking major grievances with the media to court, leaders of organizations should carefully weigh the value of making a point versus the potential downside of dragging out the issue in public.

CHAPTER 15

Metrics in Media Relations: The Importance of Tracking One's Efforts

Good businesspeople strive to comprehend what they'll receive before they buy something. They want to know the return on investment (or ROI). Likewise, leaders of companies and nonprofits should have clear expectations about any media relations campaign they intend to implement.

To begin, determine what success looks like for any campaign. Is your objective simply to increase awareness of the company within the community? (That's usually fairly easy to get.) Or is your goal more specific, like a 20 percent increase in incoming calls inquiring about products?

Make sure you use your goals to measure the results of your company's campaigns, and put those statistics to work. They'll provide the basis for comparisons that determine the success of your upcoming campaign.

You won't find one simple way to evaluate campaign success, but a number of techniques that media relations professionals use can be helpful.

Impressions

Almost every media outlet—including newspapers, radio, TV and Internet news sites—has a rough idea of how many people they attract. Many newspapers, for instance, are closely watched by the Alliance for Audited Media (AAM), which offers the industry's source for audited media data. Through the AAM, one can find an array of verified readership, circulation, subscriber demographics, and digital activity metrics for North America's leading content providers.

The difficulty arises in obtaining a precise fix on the value of an impression. An impression means only that someone had an opportunity to see a story, not that the individual read it or viewed it.

Impressions are especially hard to evaluate when a news release is sent out to media through a regional or national press release distribution system like Business Wire or PR Newswire. A number of news websites automatically repost those releases, causing the number of impressions to jump dramatically.

Receiving circulation numbers for publications in which a story appeared poses similar questions.

While everyone who accessed the publication had the possibility of seeing the story, the reality is that the likelihood of a story being read declines if it does not appear on the front page. Additionally, statistics regarding readership of secondary pages are hard to acquire. Interestingly, most newspapers that have a pretty reliable estimate of the numbers who read the financial and sports pages typically won't provide that information.

Clipping Services

A longstanding staple of media evaluation, clipping services go through hundreds of publications to determine which ones ran an article based on the company's outreach. Years ago, clients received actual newspaper articles by mail each month. While the old-fashioned delivery method is still possible, especially when smaller publications are involved, clips are much more likely to be sent by email. Clipping services typically include the circulation figures for the publications that ran the particular clip, giving some idea of its reach.

Video clipping services are also available but relatively expensive, so they are most often used only to gauge a particular event rather than an entire campaign. For web-based stories, Google Alerts and other easily implemented monitoring systems use key word searches to provide notifications when a story runs.

Advertising Valuation Equivalency (AVE)

AVE is a simple, if somewhat misleading, method of placing a dollar value on a news story. The simple measure determines length of a story in inches or airtime, which is then compared to the cost of a comparably sized ad in the same publication or broadcast. The misleading component is the technique's failure to account for the story's impact. A positive story, for example, could be worth much more than the cost of a similar-sized ad.

Story/Campaign Evaluation

The more difficult questions to answer in assessing a media campaign are strictly interpretive:

- Did the story place the organization in a positive light? How positive?

- Did the story convey key messages accurately?

- Did the story receive prominent placement during the news broadcast or on the newspaper or web page?

- Did the organization achieve its goal for the particular outreach effort?

In-house evaluations are the toughest because of internal biases regarding the organization's products or services. Media professionals, in fact, often face clients who have high expectations for media campaigns that do not coincide with the realities of news stories.

You won't get a clear assessment of your media campaign if you're overly positive or too negative.

Ed Van Herik

I worked with an energy holding company in which one executive became terribly upset unless every reference in a story reflected well on the business. In his view, if he was featured in a story that presented ten positive observations and one cautionary or skeptical comment, only the latter counted. Another executive in the same company saw only the positive when he contributed to stories, which convinced him he was a terrific spokesman.

Clearly, an outside assessment of the coverage, preferably from someone who is familiar with the news media, places the reporting in perspective. If appropriate, a professional also suggests next steps. A solid benchmark for appraising the campaign is also important, so the process must begin by determining upfront what "success" looks like.

As a practical matter, no single method provides a comprehensive assessment of an individual media relations campaign. By combining several approaches, however, you can gather a fairly accurate determination of what a campaign's impact is and could be. Importantly, organizations that define realistic goals develop the most effective campaigns, and when a campaign underway seems to be going miserably, a good review will provide a solid basis for pulling the plug or changing direction.

Key Points:

- The most effective media campaigns are designed and evaluated with realistic expectations in mind.

- Organizations can best evaluate the impact of a media campaign by using a variety of techniques.

- The number of impressions indicates how many people had the opportunity to see a story, but the figure does not reveal insights about the level of engagement audiences had with the piece.

- Clipping services send actual or emailed copies of articles from the various publications in which they appeared along with circulation figures for the publications that ran the particular piece.

- Advertising Valuation Equivalency (AVE) measures stories in inches or air time and then compares that space to the cost of an ad of about the same size in the same publication or broadcast.

- Since an organization's executives struggle to remain unbiased in determining whether or not a campaign is successful, a more effective approach is to appoint a neutral media professional to evaluate results and offer the best next-step strategies and tactics, including the possibility of pulling the campaign.

CHAPTER 16

In-House or Outsource?

A fundamental PR question among organizations is whether to create a campaign with internal staff or hire an outside professional. The discussion often begins with the budget. While accounting for all resources, human and monetary, the plan should allow for a campaign of at least six months—the amount of time needed to make a dent in the thousands of other messages that target audiences receive daily.

As a rule, don't expect to make a difference without spending four figures or more each month, whether that's part of an employee's salary or outside consultant's fees, when accounting for all related media relations expenses. Whoever handles public relations will need to be involved in picking topics for stories, drafting talking points, creating a list of journalists to pitch, and keeping on top of media contacts—tasks that consume a minimum of several hours each week. All of that is in addition to maintaining adequate visuals for TV and print, and managing the back-and-forth discussions over story details and interview setup.

Debbie Graham Fitzgerald

To garner one quality media hit, your media relations professional could readily spend three hours upfront—pitching a reporter, coordinating an interview time, preparing and discussing the talking points with client, and passing along visuals to the reporter to support the story. Add an additional hour to oversee the media interview and another for travel—and bam!—it's easily a five-hour project.

The employee who does a good job of posting content to social media is not necessarily the person you want to put in charge of PR. Pitching to media is only half of the equation; obtaining results requires knowledge of media relations as well as a good working relationship within the company.

If you don't have the budget or inclination to hire a full-time PR professional for your organization, then consider contracting a consultant.

You can use the same procedures to evaluate potential media consultants as you would for any other specialty. First, check their credentials:

- What is their background?

- Are they knowledgeable about working the media? How did they get that way?

- Who are some of their clients? Do they have references?

- Do they specialize in helping companies in your industry? Is that important?

- Will they take some time to discuss your individual needs before signing a contract?

- How well will their working style mesh with yours?

Key Points:

- When drafting a PR budget that determines whether you will pursue a media campaign with internal staff or an outside professional, your estimated expenditures should reflect a plan that invests at least six months in your PR effort.

- If the work will be performed in-house, make certain the designated employee has sufficient time to accomplish every required task.

- Social media specialists do not necessarily possess the insights or skills to be successful in pitching to the media.

- An outside consultant could be optimal if your organization lacks the resources to hire a full-time PR professional.

CHAPTER 17

Getting Into the Game: The Cost-Capabilities Equation

Compared to advertising, PR is a low-budget item. The investment, nevertheless, can be significant. Rates can be open to negotiation and they range quite a bit among respectable PR professionals, but their charges typically run from $100 to $750 an hour. Higher rates are also not uncommon.

In part, charges are based on the size of the PR organization. A large PR firm, as in a multinational group, will incur huge overhead costs with dozens of departments and hundreds of assistants. High expenses, in turn, will be reflected in high fees.

With lower fixed costs, mid-size firms tend to have more flexible rates, but they sometimes lack the ability to serve particular market niches.

Finally, small firms, dozens of which exist in any city, run the leanest operations, often with one to three employees. Frequently, a senior-level skilled PR practitioner leads the team with expertise he or she acquired from working for a larger firm before deciding to be his or her own boss. Not surprisingly, then, small firms usually charge noticeably lower rates than medium or large PR agencies.

No matter the size of the firm you choose, count on a minimum investment of 15 hours of work each month. When taking you on as a new client, in fact, the agency could demand double the amount of time to ramp up efforts. As a result, assuming the lowest hourly rate, you would incur at least $1,500 per month to make a minimum impression; therefore, count on $1,500 going quickly, especially in the beginning.

Beyond dollars and cents, the type of PR support you require is the most important consideration. Will you need a large agency that can blanket key markets in the U.S. and abroad? Do you simply want stories in the local weeklies? Does the agency need to be familiar with your industry? Determining the answers before you begin shopping for an agency saves everyone time and effort.

Before you decide to hire any agency, obtain proposals from several firms that include estimated costs, certainly if your investment will exceed $5,000 a month. Most agencies will provide a standard plan with some details about your particular company and PR needs, but don't expect a fully fleshed out document. That will come after you reach an agreement.

Key Points:

- PR professionals typically charge in the range of $100 to $750 an hour, but higher rates are not uncommon.

- Since most organizations will require minimum investment of 15 hours of work each month for a minimal media impact, a starting PR budget would be at least $1,500 per month. Rates vary relative to the size of a firm because of overhead, but in addition to considering costs, organizations need to assess their needs in light of contending PR agencies' capabilities, including their ability to penetrate overseas and/or niche markets.

- Before settling on an agency, prospective clients should request proposals that compare costs and competencies.

CHAPTER 18

Getting the Most From a Media Relations Professional

Successful relationships depend on each party contributing optimally to meet mutually acknowledged goals. Media relations professionals, therefore, expect the following from their clients:

- **Communication.** Utilize the professional as a trusted adviser and communicate openly with her or him. Be honest, factual and ethical in your communications at all times.

- **Access.** Provide the best way for you to be reached at a moment's notice. The media often need information quickly, so their ability to contact you in a timely manner is critical.

- **Quick responses.** Be prepared to return calls and answer questions promptly. The same is true for reviewing press release drafts or other copy for accuracy and clarity within the time frame requested.

- **Be proactive.** Don't just wait for your media relations pro to call you. Initiate calls to announce your organization's latest news—new services and products, new hires, new clients, charity contributions, mergers and acquisitions, industry trends, fresh insights, and new legislation coming down the pike.

Debbie Graham Fitzgerald

A client of mine contacted me early one morning to talk about a breaking TV news story he saw the night before. He had expertise to comment on the story, so I pitched the idea to the same news station that broke the story. That day, a TV reporter interviewed my client in his office for his professional opinion on the matter, and the story ran on the six o'clock news that night. Now that's what I call successful teamwork!

Ed Van Herik

When opportunity knocks, move immediately to open the door. Once, while I was working for a major nonprofit in Atlanta, a TV station called, asking for a quick interview on the nonprofit's area of expertise. Within 90 minutes, I had written the talking points, briefed the state director, and had him outside the building, in front of a camera. The interview ran that night.

Key Points:

- Treat your PR professional as a part of your inner team. Their insights will help you shape your decisions and your messages for maximum effectiveness.

- Remember, speed is of the essence in media relations. Get back to your PR person quickly when they call; a postponed opportunity is usually one that is lost.

CHAPTER 19

Making a Commitment to Media Relations

Perhaps the biggest changes in media relations in the last five years have been the growth of communications channels and the acceleration of the news cycle. Where once companies had a few hours—at least—to consider their response to a crisis, now the time is often just minutes. And sometimes, a good opportunity for media coverage doesn't last much longer than that.

The speedup in the news cycle is one of the reasons why the field of Public Relations is now listed as one of the top 10 most stressful professions in America. That stepped-up pace correspondingly presents implications

Ed Van Herik

It pays to be nimble. Once, while I was working for a utility in the Southwest, we got a call that a hawk seemed to be entangled in overhead lines. I went to the site and confirmed that the bird was twisted in the wires and appeared in pain, about 30 feet up. I consulted with a vice president and a district manager, and they arranged to send over a bucket truck. We went up in the bucket, untangled the bird, and got a huge photo in the morning newspaper of the rescue.

for companies that are considering a foray into public relations in general and media relations in particular.

Today's news intensity places a premium on the ability to size up an opportunity quickly and respond appropriately. Paradoxically, successful interchanges today are often born from painstaking work done by companies and their PR people weeks and sometimes months in advance.

It is much easier to respond quickly if you've spent time up front thinking through your positions, creating short talking points and practicing your delivery. If most of the thought process has already been completed and "in the can," then a busy executive and his PR team are, in effect, only reviewing a bit of new information before deciding how to respond to an event.

Being prepared is also essential because the implications of what you say are more widespread. With a proliferation of news channels, not to mention individual blogs and neighborhood newsletters, the chance that a company or nonprofit will come up for public scrutiny is increasing. We've found that it is much easier to be seen as a credible and responsible member of the community when the basics of PR are built into the organization's DNA.

PR professionals are trained to view activities as the media and the public will view them. By having them at the table as key decisions are being considered, an organization is prepping itself for an expanded role in business and the community.

Too often, the opposite happens: We've seen product teams proudly unveil their product to their publicity team after a year of toiling over the new product. At that point, despite all of the effort they've invested, they suddenly find out that a significant shift in presentation is necessary to catch the public's attention. Don't be that organization!

As executives calculate when and if to enter into the media relations world, they would also do well to consider other aspects of marketing. Many marketing agencies, which typically have relied on advertising to promote their clients, are joining with public relations and social media agencies to present a comprehensive communications package to their clients. That has long been the case with the largest agencies, but the practice is now becoming the norm for mid-size firms as well.

In this book, we focused on media relations because of its high-risk, high-visibility nature. If a company fumbles that aspect of outreach, recovery can take an extremely long time, if even possible. That being said, organizations should neither be fearful of pursuing media relations, nor they should focus only on PR. A combination of PR and other marketing activities can be significant contributors to the bottom line.

Finally, we wrote this book because media relations is not intuitively obvious; it takes skill and savvy to succeed. The best PR professionals are smart, driven and customer-oriented. They are knowledgeable about their industry and they look forward to learning from and about others. And while they'll charge you for their time promoting your organization, they won't charge you for the time they need to learn about it. Optimistic and willing to dig in, they are genuinely excited to see their clients succeed.

Look for the same qualities when selecting a PR person, whether you hire an employee to work from the inside or an external agency to become an extension of your organization. Either way, you now have some basic rules and insights to pick players for your PR team. Get ready to play an exciting yet respectable game with an approach that best suits your goals to expand your organization through the media.

May the megaphones be with you!